NAVIGATING DIGITAL ASSETS THE CRYPTO MARKET

THE INVESTOR'S GUIDE TO DIGITAL ASSETS

PREFACE

Welcome to "Navigating Digital Assets & the Crypto Market." In the ever- evolving landscape of finance and investments, digital assets and cryptocurrencies have emerged as transformative forces. As the world undergoes a digital revolution, understanding these new financial instruments is essential for anyone seeking to grow their wealth and embrace the future of finance.

This book is the culmination of my passion for digital assets, blockchain technology, and investment strategies. Drawing from my experiences and insights gained throughout my career, I aim to provide you with a comprehensive guide to this exciting and dynamic field.

The journey we embark on within these pages is one of exploration, education, and empowerment. Whether you are a seasoned investor looking to diversify your portfolio or someone new to the world of cryptocurrencies, this book is designed to be your reliable companion. It is my hope that by the end of this journey, you will not only have a deeper understanding of digital assets but also the confidence to navigate the crypto market with clarity and purpose.

Each chapter in this book delves into a specific aspect of digital assets and blockchain technology, from understanding the fundamentals to exploring the risks, taxation, and regulation. We'll also look at real-world applications and the potential future developments in this ever-evolving space.

The financial world is changing rapidly, and this book is your guide to staying ahead of the curve. My goal is to empower you with the knowledge and tools necessary to make informed investment choices and seize the opportunities presented by digital assets.

I invite you to join me on this enlightening journey into the realm of digital finance and cryptocurrency investments. Whether you are an individual investor, a financial professional, or simply someone curious about the future of finance, there is something here for you. Let's embark on this educational adventure together and embrace the exciting potential that digital assets offer.

Thank you for choosing "Navigating Digital Assets & the Crypto Market." I am excited to be your guide as we explore this fascinating and transformative landscape.

Cas Havis II

CONTENTS

UNDERSTANDING BLOCKCHAIN TECHNOLOGY

Explanation of Blockchain Technology and its Components

Blockchain is a distributed digital ledger system of recording information that makes it difficult to change, manipulate, or hack.[1] Imagine blockchain as a digital ledger of transactions that is duplicated and distributed across the entire network of computer systems that is tamper-proof. Unlike a regular database or ledger where one central authority manages and controls all the data, a blockchain allows many people or entities to maintain and update the records collectively. The decentralization makes blockchain more secure and reliable than a regular database or ledger.

As a type of distributed ledger technology (DLT), blockchain has all the transactions recorded with an immutable cryptographic signature known as a **hash**.

What it means is that whenever a change is made on a block within the chain, all the participants are informed that the network has been tampered with. If bad actors such as hackers wanted to tamper with or corrupt a blockchain network, they would have to change every block in the chain, across all of the distributed versions of the chain.

To understand blockchain technology even better, picture a spreadsheet that is duplicated multiple times across a network of computers. At the same time, users are informed of every update on the network, making it easy for users to track all the activities on the network. In other words, the records are public and verifiable. More importantly, since the data is distributed across multiple locations, it's harder to hack, hence more secure.

Graphical illustration of blockchain features

---

1   H. Sternberg and G. Baruffaldi, "Chains in chains: Logic and challenges of blockchains in supply chains," in Proceedings of the 51st Annual Hawaii International Conference on System Sciences 2018 (HICSS-51), pp. 3936–3943, 2018.

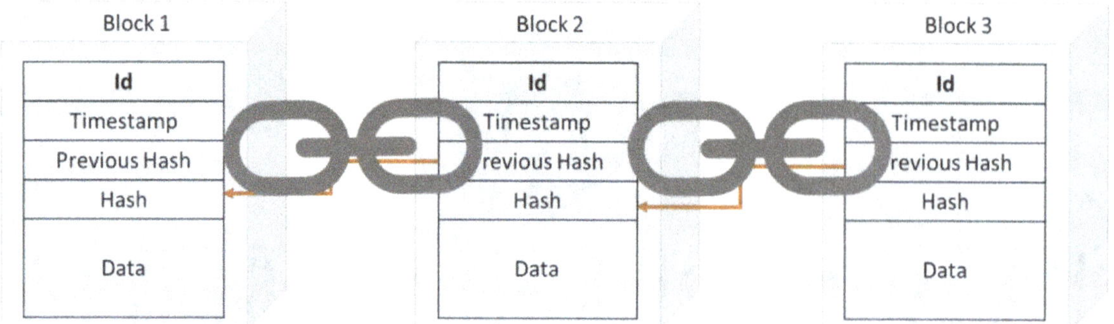

So, how does blockchain work?

- *Blocks*: a block represents a piece of information (data) with information like transactions, ownership details, and any other relevant information.

- *Chain*: These blocks are now connected to one another in a structure resembling a chain. The previous block's code is included in each block, along with its own special code (hash). With the help of this chaining, it is made sure that the data is stable and cannot be changed easily.

- *Consensus*: All members of the blockchain network must concur that the data is accurate before adding a new block to the chain. Consensus-building techniques are used to reach this consensus, which guarantees that only true and legitimate information is added.

- *Security*: Because each block is connected to every other block in the chain before it and after it, it is very difficult to change the data once it is added to the chain. Due to the required computational power and the distributed nature of the blockchain, changing information in one block would necessitate changing information in every subsequent block, which is practically impossible.

- *Decentralization*: As opposed to traditional systems, in which a single entity is in charge of all the data, a blockchain is a network of many computers (or "nodes") that share the same data. Since there is no single point of vulnerability, it is more resistant to failures and attacks as a result of decentralization.

- *Applications:* Blockchain technology has a wide range of uses, with cryptocurrencies being one of the most well-known ones. Blockchain is a technology used by cryptocurrencies to track transactions and confirm the ownership of digital assets like Bitcoin. Blockchain technology is also being investigated for supply chain management, voting systems, identity verification, and other applications.

In essence, a blockchain is similar to a digital, open, and unchangeable ledger that is maintained by a group of users rather than a single authority. In numerous applications across various industries, it provides transparency, security, and trust.

Overview of Blockchain's Impact on Various Industries

While blockchain was initially viewed as a general-purpose technology that further increases productivity, it has emerged to change multiple industries, including industrial organizations.[2]

By providing transparent, secure, and decentralized solutions, blockchain technology has emerged as a disruptive force, revolutionizing numerous industries. Blockchain is fundamentally a distributed ledger that securely and irreversibly logs transactions or data, ensuring that once data is added, it cannot be changed or removed without agreement from network users. Industries that depend on data integrity, trust, and accountability must consider this characteristic. Let's look at some significant industries, such as supply chain, and see how blockchain has affected them.

Supply chain Management:

Blockchain has significantly improved transparency and traceability throughout the entire supply chain, which has a significant impact on supply chain management. Stakeholders can easily trace products from their place of origin to their destination by recording every transaction and movement of goods on the blockchain. This lowers the possibility of fraud and counterfeiting and guarantees the genuineness of the goods. Furthermore, the automated execution of contracts made possible by smart contracts deployed on the blockchain promotes more efficient operations, less paperwork, and quicker dispute resolution.

Banking and finance:

The introduction of cryptocurrencies and decentralized finance (DeFi) platforms by blockchain disrupted the financial industry. As alternate money and exchange systems, cryptocurrencies like Bitcoin and Ethereum have emerged. The decentralized nature of blockchain eliminates the need for middlemen in transactions, potentially lowering transaction costs and increasing financial inclusion, particularly in areas with limited access to traditional banking services.

---

2   H. Wu, Z. Li, B. King, Z. Ben Miled, J. Wassick, and J. Tazelaar, "A distributed ledger for supply chain physical distribution visibility," Information, vol. 8, no. 4, p. 137, 2017

Healthcare:

By addressing issues with data security and interoperability, blockchain is revolutionizing the healthcare sector. The confidentiality and accessibility of patients are guaranteed by medical records stored on the blockchain, which also upholds the integrity of the data. This makes it possible for patient data to be seamlessly shared between various healthcare providers, enhancing care coordination and lowering medical errors. Blockchain-based solutions are also used in pharmaceutical supply chain management to fight fake medicines.

Real Estate:

Through the use of tokenization and smart contracts, blockchain is upending the real estate sector. Real estate investments are now more accessible to a wider range of investors thanks to tokenization, which enables fractional ownership of properties. Smart contracts streamline property transfers and lessen reliance on middlemen like title companies by automating and enforcing contractual obligations.

Intellectual property:

A secure and open method of managing intellectual property rights is provided by blockchain technology. On the blockchain, creators can timestamp their works to establish ownership and copyright proof. In addition to ensuring proper attribution and payment for creative content, this helps prevent unauthorized use.

Voting and Governance:

Voting records in blockchain-based systems are more transparent and unalterable. Election results can be manipulated less easily by bad actors by decentralizing the voting process. By enhancing democratic procedures and boosting public confidence in government, this technology has the potential to be beneficial.

Supply Chain:

Blockchain is essential for tracking the origin and movement of goods and raw materials, in addition to the earlier discussion of supply chain management. In industries like fashion and luxury goods, where counterfeiting is a serious problem, companies can use blockchain to verify the authenticity and ethical sourcing of products.

Energy:

Peer-to-peer energy trading, which allows people and businesses to directly buy and sell excess energy from renewable sources, is one way that blockchain is upending the energy industry. By fostering a more decentralized and sustainable energy ecosystem, blockchain lessens reliance on conventional energy suppliers.

The potential for change is enormous, but overall, the impact of blockchain on different industries is still in its early stages. We can anticipate even more creative use cases that will revolutionize the way these industries function and offer services as the technology develops and becomes more widely adopted. Scalability, regulatory compliance, and public perception issues still need to be resolved for blockchain to fully realize its potential across industries.

Explanation of Consensus Mechanisms

If you're just getting started with cryptocurrency trading, it's imperative that you understand the fundamentals of blockchain consensus.

Typically, when a group decides by consensus, it means that the majority of the group (nodes) supports it. The percentage of nodes that constitutes a majority depends on each network. For example, Ethereum concludes that a consensus has been reached when 66% of the nodes agree with a decision.[3] The objectives of a consensus are to ensure an agreement is reached to collaborate and cooperate, nodes enjoy equal rights, and mandatory participation of each node in the process of consensus.

Consensus is crucial in fostering trust among cryptocurrency traders all over the world. Due to the decentralized nature of the cryptocurrency industry, complete transparency is crucial when trading a particular coin. A buyer's chances of falling victim to fraud are reduced as a result. It also prevents double-spending and ensures the integrity and immutability of the distributed ledger.

This brings us to what is known as a consensus mechanism, which is defined as a system that validates a transaction and marks it as authentic. All valid transactions of a coin in a blockchain are listed in a blockchain to build trust in the coin among traders. Many cryptocurrencies, including Bitcoin and Ethereum, use consensus mechanisms to ensure the security of their networks. The blockchain's security is upheld by the consensus mechanism, which keeps track of all legal transactions.

Due to the decentralized nature of cryptocurrency trading, this is crucial to prevent sellers from purposefully defrauding buyers. The consensus mechanism makes sure that a transaction is reflected in the blockchain as soon as it is validated, which helps to establish trust for a blockchain. A blockchain network must implement several methodologies to guarantee security, build trust, and reach consensus. Consensus mechanisms also make sure that all of a coin's transactions are accurately recorded in the blockchain.

What are the types of consensus mechanisms?

---

3   https://ethereum.org/en/developers/docs/consensus-mechanisms/

'Consensus Mechanism' is a term often used colloquially to refer to 'proof-of-stake', 'proof-of-work, or 'proof-of-authority' protocols. However, a consensus mechanism can be broadly described as a complete stack of ideas, protocols, and incentives that enable a distributed set of nodes (network users) to agree on the state of a blockchain.

Advantages of Consensus Mechanisms

A consensus mechanism can offer numerous advantages, including:

- Lowering the barrier to participation: any crypto trader or miner from anywhere around the globe can participate in a consensus mechanism

- Building trust among users: miners and traders of a particular crypto asset across the globe must agree to approve a decision, which in turn can build trust among users.

- Establishing security: it ensures transparency of trading for all coins; thus, traders can ensure that no fraud occurs during a transaction.

Consensus Mechanism Applications in Supply Chain Management

Consensus mechanism is increasingly being applied across many industries, including the supply chain industry. Some of the top companies using blockchain's consensus mechanism are Walmart, BMW, AMEX, Amazon, Maersk, Coca-Cola, and Unilever, among others.

1. Walmart: the retail chain uses blockchain technology to trace its food supply chain. They have a system based on blockchain that helps them know where their food products come from and how they move through the supply chain.

2. Amazon: Amazon employs blockchain technology for a safer and faster payment system. Their blockchain-based payment system can process transactions more efficiently and securely compared to traditional methods.

3. Maersk: Maersk, a global shipping company, utilizes blockchain technology to streamline its shipping processes. They have a platform that tracks shipments and shares real-time data with customers.

4. Coca-Cola: Coca-Cola utilizes blockchain to track the movement of its ingredients. Their blockchain-based system helps them trace the origin and movement of ingredients through the supply chain.

5. Unilever: Unilever employs blockchain to create a platform for tracking the sustainability of its products. Consumers can verify the sustainability of Unilever products and track their journey from source to store.

6. American Express (AMEX): AMEX developed the blockchain technology solution, Hyperledger Fabric, to use to manage the reward system and keep customers' card details private and secure.

7. Maersk: the logistics firm is using blockchain technology's consensus mechanism to provide customs officials with real-time access to shipping data, reducing delays and increasing efficiency.

8. Mitsubishi: The Japanese logistics giant has harnessed the power blockchain consensus mechanism to enable clients to track outsourced pharmaceutical shipments, as a way to guarantee the products are kept under proper conditions throughout the shipping process.

These are just but a few examples of how blockchain technology's consensus mechanism has become useful in the supply chain industry. Consensus mechanism is an excellent tool for a decentralized form of transactions due to the critical features of decentralization, programmability, security, immutability, anonymity, and its ability to be time-stamped.

02

TYPES OF DIGITAL ASSETS

Overview of Cryptocurrencies, Tokens, and Stablecoins

Before we delve into the world of crypto trading, let's dive into what it is, its features, and how it works.

You have most likely heard about Bitcoin or other cryptocurrencies such as Ethereum and Dogecoin. Either a friend, family member, workmate, neighbor, or your Uber driver, narrated to you how they made lots of money buying and selling Bitcoin, Dogecoin, Ethereum, or some other lesser-known cryptocurrency.

But how do you get to understand the nitty-gritty of cryptocurrency and what it takes to trade them? This is a question that continues to pop up everywhere among curious individuals who would want to get into crypto trading. So, in this section, we are going to walk you through the basics of digital asset types, and how it works.

Cryptocurrencies (or simply Crypto) have become increasingly popular alternative currencies for online payments. At the same time, some terms such as tokens and stablecoins have increasingly dominated the world of cryptocurrency enthusiasts.

Cryptocurrency is a digital asset, which is an alternative form of payment that is decentralized, based on blockchain technology, and secured by cryptography. It can also be referred to as an electronic peer-to-peer currency.

The most well-known cryptocurrency is Bitcoin, which was created in 2009 by an anonymous person going by the pseudo-name *Satoshi Nakamoto*. Bitcoin's success paved the way for the emergence of numerous other cryptocurrencies, collectively referred to as altcoins.

One of the most obvious features of cryptocurrency (digital asset) is that you can't physically hold it. However, this does not mean that they lack value as you have noticed how rapidly Bitcoin and other thousands of cryptocurrencies have risen in prices over the last decade. Moreover, there has been an astronomical rise in the number of cryptocurrencies in the market. As of July 2023, there were more than 23,000 cryptocurrencies, according to CoinMarketCap.com.

Let's unpack some of the important features of a digital asset:

- Digital form: digital assets are only available in electronic form, unlike conventional currencies (e.g., USD, Yen, Euro, etc.) that are issued and regulated by governments. They are electronically stored and managed on computer systems rather than being actual coins or bills.

- Decentralized: Cryptocurrencies are decentralized in nature. The decentralization feature distinguishes it from conventional currencies such as USD that are governed by centralized entities such as a bank or a government. Instead, cryptocurrencies run on a decentralized computer network known as blockchain (discussed in *Chapter 1*).

- Secured through cryptography: To secure transactions and regulate the creation of new units, cryptocurrencies use cryptographic techniques. Only the cryptocurrency's owner may transfer it, thanks to the use of cryptographic keys by network participants to sign transactions. Because of this, cryptocurrencies are very safe and fraud-resistant. Each cryptocurrency user has a set of cryptographic keys, known as a public key and a private key. While the user's private key is kept private and is used to sign transactions, proving ownership of the cryptocurrency, the public key acts as an address for receiving payments from others.

- The process of creating new units is known as "mining" in some cryptocurrencies, such as Bitcoin. Individuals or organizations known as miners use powerful computers to solve challenging mathematical puzzles, validating transactions and adding them to the blockchain as a result. Miners are given newly created cryptocurrency units as payment for their work.

- Pseudonymity: Cryptocurrency transactions offer some degree of privacy because they are not directly connected to real-world identities. User identities are instead represented by their distinctive cryptographic addresses. It's important to keep in mind, though, that certain blockchain transactions or activities may be examined to infer user identities.

- Cross-border Transactions: Because cryptocurrencies are borderless, they enable quick and affordable global transactions without the use of middlemen like banks. In relation to international transfers, this feature is especially helpful.

- Volatility: The price of digital assets can be extremely volatile, meaning that they can change considerably in a short amount of time. For investors and users, this volatility may present both opportunities and risks.

In general, cryptocurrencies present an innovative and different way to conduct financial transactions, creating a financial system that is currently disrupting traditional financial systems. However, users should use caution, do extensive research, and implement appropriate security measures when dealing with cryptocurrencies.

Tokens:

Tokens are types of digital assets (cryptocurrencies) that are built on top of existing blockchain platforms like Ethereum, Binance Smart Chain, or others. Unlike traditional cryptocurrencies, which have their own native blockchain, tokens rely on the underlying blockchain's infrastructure for their operation. Tokens can represent various assets, such as digital assets, real-world assets, utility access, or even voting rights within a decentralized organization.

Tokens are created through smart contracts, which are self-executing contracts with predefined rules. Smart contracts facilitate the issuance, distribution, and management of tokens. The most popular standard for tokens on the Ethereum blockchain is the ERC-20 standard, but there are other standards like ERC-721 for non-fungible tokens (NFTs) and ERC-1155 for hybrid fungible/non-fungible tokens.

Stablecoins:

Stablecoins are a type of cryptocurrency that aims to maintain a stable value, often pegged to a reserve of assets like fiat currencies (e.g., US Dollar, Euro) or commodities (e.g., gold). The idea behind stablecoins is to mitigate the price volatility common in many cryptocurrencies, making them more suitable for everyday transactions and as a store of value. Stability is achieved through various mechanisms, such as collateralization, algorithmic adjustments, or a combination of both.

The main purpose of stablecoins is to provide the benefits of cryptocurrencies (fast and borderless transactions) while minimizing the price volatility often associated with traditional cryptocurrencies like Bitcoin or Ethereum. Stablecoins find widespread use in the cryptocurrency space for trading, remittances, and as a store of value during market downturns. Tether (USDT) is one of the well-known stablecoins that is pegged to the value of the US dollar. It works in such a way that for each USDT in circulation, there should be an equivalent value of US dollars held in reserve to back its value.

Explanation of Utility Tokens, Security Tokens, and Non-Fungible Tokens (NFTs)

Tokens refer to a type of digital asset that exists on a blockchain platform such as Ethereum and Polygon. They are programmable units of value that represent various assets or utilities. As earlier explained, tokens are different from cryptocurrencies such as Bitcoin, which have their own native blockchain. This is because tokens are created and hosted on existing blockchain networks using smart contracts. These smart contracts define the rules and functionalities of the token, including its supply, distribution, and behavior.

Tokens can serve multiple purposes in the crypto ecosystem. Some tokens act as digital representations of real-world assets, such as real estate or precious metals, providing fractional ownership and increased liquidity. Others function as utility tokens, granting access to specific services or products within a blockchain-based platform. Additionally, there are security tokens, which represent ownership in a company and are subject to relevant financial regulations. The popularity of tokens has led to the rise of Initial Coin Offerings (ICOs) and other token sale mechanisms, allowing projects to raise funds by selling their tokens to investors in exchange for cryptocurrencies like Bitcoin or Ethereum. As a result, tokens play a crucial role in enabling innovative blockchain-based projects and shaping the decentralized economy.

There are various types of tokens, each with its own specific characteristics and use cases. However, in the scope of this book, we'll discuss the most popular tokens in Utility tokens, security tokens, and non-fungible tokens (NFTs).

i. *Utility Tokens:* Utility tokens are cryptocurrencies that provide access to specific products, services, or functionalities within a blockchain-based platform. They are often used to facilitate interactions and transactions within decentralized applications (DApps) and ecosystems. Utility tokens are not considered investments, and their value is typically linked to the demand for the services they enable. They do not represent ownership or equity in the underlying project.

   Utility tokens can be used to facilitate access services, internal currencies, decentralized governance, token burning, and ICOs and token sales. To avoid being classified as a security and to comply with regulations, utility tokens must primarily serve a practical utility or function within the platform, rather than primarily existing as an investment vehicle.

   Featuring prominently in this token category are Ethereum's native cryptocurrency, Ether (ETH), and Binance's Binance Coin (BSC). These utility tokens are used to pay transaction fees and execute smart contracts on the Ethereum Network.

ii. *Security Tokens:*

Security tokens are digital tokens that represent ownership in a traditional asset, such as real estate, equity, or debt. Unlike utility tokens, security tokens are considered financial securities and are subject to regulations set forth by financial authorities in various jurisdictions. They can provide token holders with rights, such as dividends, voting power, or profit-sharing, similar to traditional securities.

Security tokens offer several advantages over traditional securities. They enable fractional ownership, allowing investors to own a portion of high-value assets, which was previously inaccessible due to high entry barriers. Additionally, security token offerings (STOs) streamline the fundraising process for businesses by reducing intermediaries, minimizing costs, and expanding the investor base globally. However, since security tokens fall under securities regulations, their issuance and trading involve compliance with applicable laws, making the process more complex than that of utility tokens. Despite the challenges, security tokens hold significant potential to revolutionize the financial markets by unlocking liquidity, enhancing market efficiency, and democratizing investment opportunities.

Some of the prominent examples of security tokens are Polymath, tZero, Harbor, and Securitize. These digital tokens represent shares of each of the company's stock. The tokens are considered security tokens because they represent ownership in the company and may entitle the token holders to dividends and voting rights.

iii. *Non-Fungible Tokens (NFTs):*

NFTs are unique digital assets that represent ownership of specific items or pieces of content. Each NFT has a distinct value and cannot be exchanged on a one-to-one basis with other tokens, unlike cryptocurrencies, which are fungible and interchangeable. NFTs are often used to represent digital art, collectibles, virtual real estate, and other unique assets. For example, an artist creates a digital artwork and mints it as an NFT on a blockchain. The NFT represents the sole ownership of that specific artwork, and it can be bought, sold, or traded on various NFT marketplaces.

CoinMarketCap.com puts NFTs' market cap at approximately $1.3 billion, and the revenue is projected to grow by 18.55% annually. Sales of some NFTs continue to surpass $1 million, as evidenced by the $1.6 million in revenue generated by *Yuga Labs'* "Golden Key" in February. A *Bored Ape* was purchased for $1.3 million, and *CryptoPunk 5066* was sold for $1.4 million. The highest NFT sale in 2022 took place for 800 ETH, or a staggering $23.7 million, and involved *CryptoPunk 5822.* Digital artist Pak's creation *Merge* currently holds the record for the most expensive NFT ever sold at US$91.8 million on the NFT platform Nifty Gateway.[4]

---

4   https://crypto.com/university/most-expensive-nfts

It's important to note that the regulatory status and classification of these tokens can vary depending on the jurisdiction, and the definitions provided here are a general overview. Before getting involved with any of these tokens, it's advisable to research the legal and regulatory considerations in your location.

Comparison of Digital Assets to Traditional Assets

Digital assets and traditional assets are two distinct categories of assets, each with its own characteristics and features. While most of us are familiar with traditional assets like bonds, stocks, and cash, digital assets are still new to the financial market as they only emerged slightly over a decade ago.

Digital assets have drawn a lot of attention in recent years due to the many benefits users have drawn over the past decade. These decentralized digital currencies have several benefits over traditional assets, including quick and affordable transactions, accessibility on a global scale, and improved security. Moreover, the blockchain technology that powers digital assets paves the way for novel applications like smart contracts and decentralized financing (DeFi) by enabling greater transparency, immutability, and programmability.

However, despite their rising popularity, digital assets still face several obstacles to widespread adoption. The lack of integration with the established banking system is one of the most important problems.

Digital assets are frequently viewed as risky, speculative, and unregulated by traditional investors and institutions. Additionally, the infrastructure that underpins digital assets, such as exchanges and custody options, is still being refined.

So, let's dive into the actual difference between these two types of assets:

i. *Nature and form*

   - Traditional assets are physical or tangible assets, such as real estate, commodities (like gold, silver), stocks, bonds, and cash. They have a physical existence and are typically regulated by traditional financial systems.

   - Digital assets: these assets are intangible assets that exist solely in digital form. Digital assets like Bitcoin, Ethereum, utility tokens, security tokens, digital art, and other non-fungible tokens (NFTs) fall under this category. They are decentralized and often based on blockchain technology.

ii. *Regulation*

   - Traditional assets: These are usually heavily regulated by government bodies and financial institutions. Various laws and regulatory frameworks are in place to govern their issuance, trading, and custody.

- Digital assets: Regulation of digital assets varies significantly from country to country. Some countries have adopted specific regulations, while others are still developing appropriate frameworks due to the relative novelty of digital assets.

iii. *Accessibility*

- Traditional assets: Access to traditional assets often requires intermediaries such as banks, brokers, or financial institutions. Transactions can be subject to fees and processing times.

- Digital assets: Digital assets provide greater accessibility and are often traded on decentralized platforms, enabling peer-to-peer transactions without the need for intermediaries. This can result in lower fees and faster settlement times.

iv. *Ownership and Custody*

- Traditional assets: Ownership of traditional assets is usually represented by physical certificates or legal documentation. Custody may involve physical storage, like a safe deposit box for precious metals, or electronic custody for securities held with a brokerage.

- Digital assets: Ownership of digital assets is represented by cryptographic keys stored in digital wallets. Custody can be self-managed through personal wallets or entrusted to third-party custodians or exchanges.

v. *Volatility and Liquidity*

- Traditional assets: While traditional assets can experience price fluctuations, their volatility is often lower compared to digital assets. Liquidity can vary depending on the asset, with some assets being highly liquid (e.g., major stocks) and others less so.

- Digital assets: Digital assets are known for their high volatility, with significant price fluctuations occurring within short periods. Liquidity can also vary widely, with major cryptocurrencies generally having higher liquidity than smaller or less-established tokens.

vi. *Market Hours*

- Traditional assets: Traditional financial markets usually operate during specific hours on business days, typically following the time zones of their respective countries.

- Digital assets: Digital asset markets are open 24/7, enabling continuous trading without any time restrictions.

vii. *Use Cases*

- Traditional assets: Traditional assets often serve as investments, stores of value, and means of generating income through dividends or interest.

- Digital assets: Digital assets can also serve as investment vehicles but have additional use cases due to their blockchain-based nature, including decentralized finance (DeFi), non-fungible tokens for digital collectibles and art, and facilitating cross-border transactions.

It's important to note that both digital assets and traditional assets have their own risks and benefits, and the suitability of each asset class depends on individual financial goals, risk tolerance, and investment strategies. Diversification across both categories may be advisable for a well-rounded investment portfolio.

THE CRYPTOCURRENCY MARKET

03

Overview of the cryptocurrency market and its volatility

Cryptocurrency has emerged as a disruptive force in the financial world, reshaping the way we perceive and conduct transactions. Devised as a decentralized alternative to traditional currencies, cryptocurrencies have rapidly gained popularity and global acceptance. Central to the cryptocurrency experience is its inherent volatility, which has been both a catalyst for immense profits and a source of trepidation for investors. This section presents an overview of the cryptocurrency market, and how its high volatility impacts market activities. It also highlights how you can embrace crypto volatility in pursuit of decentralized investment opportunities.

Exploring Crypto Market Volatility: Understanding the Risks and Rewards

Market volatility is a prominent characteristic of cryptocurrencies, with significant price fluctuations leading to both potential gains and losses. This aspect has made the crypto market a challenging environment for investors who prefer stability. To navigate this landscape successfully, crypto investors must remain agile and adaptable to the constantly changing market dynamics.

What Does Crypto Market Volatility Mean?

Volatility refers to the rapidity with which prices can change. The world of cryptocurrencies is closely associated with volatility due to frequent and substantial fluctuations in their prices.

It's important to recognize that not all cryptocurrencies exhibit the same level of volatility. The degree of volatility varies significantly depending on the asset in question. For instance, well-established cryptocurrencies like Bitcoin and Ethereum typically have lower volatility compared to newly-launched meme coins. Generally, the higher the volatility of a cryptocurrency, the riskier the investment becomes. On the other hand, a less volatile token may offer more stable returns but at the cost of potentially lower gains.

The Factors Contributing to Crypto Market Volatility

The crypto market's relatively short existence of just over a decade contributes to its high volatility compared to traditional markets like stocks and bonds. Established large-cap stocks such as Apple (AAPL) and Microsoft (MSFT) in the stock market tend to be less erratic compared to smaller tech stocks that showcase a broader range of volatility. Bonds, known for their low volatility, are often favored by conservative investors seeking safety in their investments over higher returns. To navigate the turbulent waters of the crypto market successfully, investors are advised to consider diversifying their portfolios. By spreading investments across different assets with varying volatility levels, they can mitigate some of the risks associated with wild price swings.

The Potential for Higher Returns

While high volatility poses risks, it also presents opportunities for potentially high returns. The crypto market's ability to experience significant price surges can result in substantial profits for those who time their investments strategically. However, investors must exercise caution and conduct thorough research before committing funds to highly volatile assets.

Balancing Risk and Reward

Ultimately, the decision to invest in cryptocurrency should be based on an individual's risk tolerance and investment goals. Some investors are more comfortable taking higher risks for the chance of substantial gains, while others prioritize stability and safety, even if it means potentially lower returns.

In summary, the crypto market's volatility is a double-edged sword, offering both risks and rewards. Understanding the nature of volatility and employing prudent investment strategies can help crypto investors navigate this exciting yet unpredictable landscape more effectively. As the market matures, it may experience reduced volatility, making it more appealing to a broader range of investors.

- Explanation of market cycles and trends

The cryptocurrency market is like a rollercoaster ride of emotions and adrenaline rushes. Just like any rollercoaster, it has its ups and downs, loops and twists, and you can bet it's going to keep your heart racing.

Market cycles and trends in the cryptocurrency market refer to the repetitive patterns and movements observed in the prices of cryptocurrencies over time.

These cycles and trends are driven by a combination of factors, including market sentiment, investor behavior, technological advancements, regulatory changes, and macroeconomic conditions. Understanding these cycles and trends can help you as an investor or a trader make more informed investment decisions. Here's a breakdown of market cycles and trends:

1. *Bull Market:*

   During a bull market, cryptocurrency prices experience a sustained upward trend. Positive news, technological advancements, and growing interest from retail and institutional investors fuel the optimism and drive prices higher. In a bull market, the overall sentiment is positive, leading to a "fear of missing out" (FOMO) mentality among investors, which further contributes to the price surge. Bull markets can last for months to years, and the price gains can be substantial.

2. *Bear Market:*

   Conversely, during a bear market, cryptocurrency prices go through a sustained period of decline. Negative news, regulatory uncertainties, security breaches, or a general cooling-off of market sentiment can trigger a bear market. As prices fall, investor confidence erodes, leading to panic selling and further price drops. Bear markets can be quite prolonged, and prices can experience significant losses.

3. *Market Consolidation:*

   After a period of either bull or bear market, a market consolidation phase may follow. In this phase, the price movements become range-bound, with the cryptocurrency trading within a relatively narrow price range. Market consolidation represents a period of indecision and typically occurs before the next major price movement.

4. *Seasonality and Cyclic Patterns:*

   Cryptocurrency markets have also shown some seasonal trends and cyclic patterns. For example, certain cryptocurrencies might experience increased demand and price appreciation at specific times of the year. These patterns could be influenced by various factors, such as holidays, tax seasons, or patterns of traditional financial markets.

5. *Long-Term Trends:*

   Beyond short-term cycles, cryptocurrencies can also exhibit long-term trends. These trends are often driven by fundamental factors, such as adoption, technological advancements, and changes in market regulations. Some cryptocurrencies may show a long-term upward trajectory due to their utility and increasing acceptance, while others might struggle to maintain relevance and lose value over time.

Market cycles and trends are crucial for crypto traders because they provide valuable insights into the price movements of cryptocurrencies over time. Understanding market cycles and trends helps traders make more informed decisions, manage risks, and potentially maximize their profits. Here are some reasons why market cycles and trends are important for crypto traders:

1. **Timing of Entry and Exit Points:** By analyzing market cycles and trends, traders can identify potential entry and exit points for their trades. Different stages of market cycles offer varying opportunities for profit. Traders can enter the market during the early stages of an uptrend (bull market) and exit before a potential downturn (bear market) begins.

2. **Risk Management:** Knowing the prevailing trend and the stage of the market cycle can help traders manage risk effectively. In bull markets, traders might take on more risk, while in bear markets, they may adopt a more defensive approach or even consider shorting strategies. Understanding market cycles assists traders in adjusting their risk exposure accordingly.

3. **Psychological and Emotional Preparedness:** Cryptocurrency markets can be highly volatile, and understanding market cycles can help traders mentally prepare for potential price swings. Recognizing that markets move in cycles can reduce panic selling during downturns and avoid excessive euphoria during bull markets.

4. **Anticipating Price Targets:** Analysis of past market cycles and trends can assist traders in predicting potential price targets for a particular cryptocurrency. Technical analysis tools, such as Fibonacci retracements and extensions, are often used to identify support and resistance levels based on historical price movements.

5. **Distinguishing Trends from Noise:** Not all price movements are part of a significant trend; some are simply short-term noise or random fluctuations. Understanding market cycles helps traders distinguish between actual trends and short-term fluctuations, enabling them to make better trading decisions.

6. **Long-term Investment Strategies:** For long-term investors, understanding market cycles can be instrumental in creating investment strategies. Identifying the early stages of a bull market can offer favorable entry points for long-term positions while recognizing the peak of a bull market might prompt investors to take profits or rebalance their portfolios.

7. **Avoiding Overtrading:** Without a grasp of market cycles and trends, traders may be tempted to overtrade or chase short-term gains. Understanding market cycles encourages a more patient and disciplined approach to trade.

8. **Market Sentiment:** Market cycles can also influence investor sentiment. Recognizing prevailing market sentiment can help traders gauge the overall mood of the market and potentially identify opportunities when sentiment reaches extreme levels (e.g., fear or greed).

In a nutshell, market cycles and trends play a crucial role in guiding crypto traders to make more informed and strategic decisions. It's important to note that the cryptocurrency market is highly speculative and can be subject to significant volatility. As such, market cycles and trends can be challenging to predict accurately. Investors should exercise caution, conduct thorough research, and consider their risk tolerance before participating in the cryptocurrency market. Additionally, regulations and market dynamics can evolve rapidly, further impacting market cycles and trends.

Discussion of market capitalization and trading volume

The crypto market is witnessing an upside momentum on the back of the global macroeconomic situation and cooling inflation data. According to Forbes, after a robust start to the year 2023, the global crypto market capitalization is trading at $1.19 trillion- a value that is expected to rise due to the ascending high trading volume.[5] Even though the trading volume is still dominated by the crypto poster boys, Bitcoin and Ethereum, there are other thousands of digital assets in the market for broader investment opportunities.

Market capitalization provides a clear picture of a cryptocurrency's standing in the market. To calculate a coin's market cap, you simply multiply the total number of coins in circulation by the price of a single coin. For instance, on August 1, 2023, Ether had a supply of 120.18 million coins. By multiplying this with its then-market price of US1,828.93, the Ethereum market cap was approximately US$220.7 billion.

Market cap is a valuable metric for comparing and ranking different coins within the crypto market. For example, let's consider the XRP, which is 52.69 billion in circulation for US$0.69. This results in a market cap of about US$37 billion. As compared to Ether's market cap, the difference is quite significant. The variation can be attributed to the fact that the two digital assets serve very different purposes. While Ripple primarily targets banks and major companies that require fast money transfer services via blockchain, Ethereum serves as both a platform for decentralized applications and as a huge smart contract base.

Market cap is subject to fluctuations based on crypto coin and token prices and their circulating supply, but the relative rankings remain relatively stable. Here are the top 10 cryptos by market cap in U.S. dollars as of Early-July 2023:

---

5   https://www.forbes.com/advisor/investing/cryptocurrency/sec-crypto-regulation/#:~:text=If%20crypto%20is%20deemed%20a,if%20cryptocurrencies%20are%20deemed%20currencies.

Rank	Crypto	Market Cap (US$)
1	Bitcoin (BTC)	570.2 billion
2	Ethereum (ETH)	224.0 billion
3	Tether (USDT)	83.8 billion
4	Ripple (XRP)	37.0 billion
5	Binance Coin (BNB)	36.6 billion
6	USD Coin (USDC)	26.5 billion
7	Dogecoin (DOGE)	11.1 billion
8	Cardano (ADA)	10.7 billion
9	Solana (SOL)	10.0 billion
10	TRON (TRX)	7.8 billion

Source: CoinMarketCap.com

Cryptocurrencies with higher market caps generally attract more investors and exert more influence over the prices of other coins and tokens. This is one of the reasons why the market cap is the standard basis for ranking cryptocurrencies within the market. Simply looking at a coin's price is insufficient; market capitalization provides a more accurate measure of its standing.

Screengrab of the BTC/USD performance as of August 1, 2023 (Source: TradeView.com)

Furthermore, the market cap can also reveal trends. For instance, if a group of cryptocurrencies related to decentralized finance applications or NFT trading experience a surge or decline in value, it signals the attraction or loss of investors in that market segment.

Trading Volume

What is Trading Volume in Cryptocurrency?

Trading volume in the context of cryptocurrencies refers to the total number of units of a crypto asset that are bought and sold across all exchanges, both centralized and decentralized, within a specific period. Each exchange typically displays its own trading volume for the asset. The volume can be measured either in US Dollars or in the units of the asset itself. For example, at the time of writing, Binance's 24-hour trading volume for BNB was either US$736.91 million selling at US$244.87 per BNB, or A circulation supply of 153.87 million BNB, according to data from CoinMarketCap.com

Trading volume is a crucial metric in the crypto market as it influences various technical indicators, including liquidity, market trends, market strength, accumulation, and market reversals.

Liquidity:

Trading volume directly affects the liquidity of an asset, which indicates how easy and fast it is to buy or sell the asset at its current market price. Higher trading volume and liquidity stabilize an asset's price and reduce frequent price fluctuations. It's important not to confuse liquidity with liquidation in crypto trading.

Market Trends:

Trading volume is essential for understanding market trends. A price move accompanied by high volume suggests the start of a strong trend. Conversely, low trading volume following a price move indicates a weak trend. A high volume during an uptrend shows high buyer interest and a willingness to push the asset's price higher. Conversely, a high volume during a downtrend indicates increasing selling pressure and low buyer interest. This relationship helps traders identify optimal entry and exit points for trades.

Market Strength:

Trading volume validates market moves. An increased volume accompanying a price change in either direction indicates a strong price move. On the other hand, if the change is accompanied by low volume, it suggests a weak change that might see a correction.

Accumulation:

Trading volume helps spot accumulation in the market. A spike in volume without a significant price movement likely indicates accumulation, meaning that high net-worth investors are gradually buying large amounts of assets. This often leads to a price surge after the accumulation phase.

Market Reversal:

A decline in trading volume despite a price movement might suggest a reversal or a price correction. For example, a price surge accompanied by low volume may indicate decreasing buying pressure and a subsequent price drop. Conversely, a price decrease accompanied by low volume signifies a decline in selling pressure and a potential price surge. However, investors should not solely rely on trading volume as a predictor of market reversal and should confirm with other technical indicators.

What Does High Volume Mean in Crypto?

High volume usually indicates high buyer interest and the potential for a price increase. In a high-volume market, assets change hands quickly and easily. However, high volume can also occur during the start or peak of a bear market when there is high selling pressure as traders anticipate a price drop. Therefore, volume should not be the sole predictor of market trends.

What Does Low Volume Mean in Crypto?

On the other hand, low volume signifies declining buyer interest, making it challenging to exchange an asset under such conditions. Low volume indicates low liquidity and falling prices. Low-volume assets tend to have low supply and can be highly volatile as their prices can be easily manipulated. For instance, a buyer can purchase a low-volume asset at a higher price to drive its price upwards and create a false uptrend, then sell it to unsuspecting investors.

How to Read Volume on a Crypto Chart?

Crypto charts typically display the volume of an asset traded within a specific time frame. You can see this information by clicking on the preferred timeframe. Candlesticks on the chart represent the volume at which a particular crypto is being traded. Longer candlesticks indicate higher volume. A green candlestick suggests buying interest, while a red candlestick indicates selling pressure. Reading crypto charts may be challenging for newer traders or those without a background in finance. We have prepared a helpful article on how to read charts like a pro, where you can learn about candlesticks, chart patterns, plotting, volume, and technical indicators.

Conclusion

The cryptocurrency market is a highly dynamic and rapidly evolving sector characterized by a wide range of digital assets like Bitcoin, Ethereum, and other altcoins. The market has experienced substantial growth and adoption over the years, attracting both institutional and retail investors. However, this growth has also been accompanied by significant volatility. Cryptocurrencies are known for their price fluctuations, which can be influenced by various factors such as regulatory developments, technological advancements, market sentiment, and macroeconomic events. This volatility presents both opportunities and risks for investors, as prices can experience rapid gains or losses within short timeframes. As the cryptocurrency market continues to mature, ongoing efforts to enhance regulation, infrastructure, and mainstream adoption may influence the level of volatility over time.

Please note that more developments are expected to take place, and it is advisable to continuously verify the latest data before making any investment decision.

04

INVESTING IN DIGITAL ASSETS

Overview of investing strategies for digital assets

In recent years, the world of finance has witnessed a remarkable shift towards digital assets, driven by the rapid advancement of blockchain technology and the increasing mainstream adoption of cryptocurrencies. Alongside the well-known cryptocurrencies such as Bitcoin and Ethereum, the trillion-dollar asset category also includes new players like non-fungible tokens (NFTs) and decentralized finance (DeFi) tokens. Valued at US$1.16 trillion, the remarkable growth has not only garnered attention from individual investors but also mainstream institutions. However, navigating this dynamic landscape requires a deep understanding of various investment strategies tailored to the unique characteristics of digital assets even as market volatility remains a defining characteristic.

In this chapter, we take you through a comprehensive overview of investing strategies in various forms of digital assets, from the investment concepts and industry terms to the most viable investment approaches every investor should consider before venturing into the business.

i. *Hodling: A Long-Term Approach*

One of the earliest and simplest strategies in the digital asset space is "hodling," derived from a misspelling of "holding." Hodlers purchase digital assets to hold onto them for an extended period, regardless of short-term market fluctuations. This approach is based on the belief that over time, the value of the asset will increase significantly, leading to substantial returns. Hodling requires patience and a strong conviction in the long-term potential of the chosen digital asset.

ii. *Day Trading: Capitalizing on Short-Term Volatility*

Day trading involves making frequent trades within a single day to take advantage of short-term price movements. This strategy requires a deep understanding of market trends, technical analysis, and real-time data interpretation. Day traders aim to profit from the volatility inherent in the digital asset markets. While potentially lucrative, day trading demands quick decision-making, discipline, and risk management skills.

iii. *Swing Trading: Riding the Waves*

Swing trading strikes a balance between hodling and day trading. Traders using this strategy seek to capitalize on medium-term price movements. They aim to enter positions at key support levels and exit when the asset's price reaches resistance levels. Swing trading requires a combination of technical and fundamental analysis, as well as a keen understanding of market sentiment.

iv. *Diversification: Spreading Risk*

Diversification involves spreading investments across a variety of digital assets, reducing the impact of poor performance on any single asset. This strategy is particularly relevant in the digital asset space due to its inherent volatility. By holding a diverse portfolio, investors can potentially mitigate risk while benefiting from the growth of multiple assets.

v. *Yield Farming and Staking: Earning Passive Income*

Yield farming and staking involve actively participating in decentralized finance (DeFi) protocols to earn rewards or interest on digital assets. Yield farmers provide liquidity to lending platforms or liquidity pools and are rewarded with interest or tokens. Stakers, on the other hand, lock up their assets to support network operations and are compensated with additional tokens. While offering potential passive income, yield farming and staking come with their own set of risks, including smart contract vulnerabilities and changes in protocol parameters.

vi. *Fundamental Analysis: Assessing Long-Term Value*

Similar to traditional investing, fundamental analysis involves evaluating the intrinsic value of digital assets based on factors such as technology, use case, team, partnerships, and market demand. This strategy aims to identify undervalued assets with strong long-term potential, regardless of short-term price fluctuations.

It's worth noting that investing in digital assets offers a plethora of opportunities but also comes with its own set of challenges and risks. The strategies mentioned above represent a spectrum of approaches that cater to different risk appetites, investment goals, and market conditions. As the digital asset space continues to mature, staying informed and adaptable will be key to making well-informed investment decisions.

Explanation of fundamental and technical analysis

There are numerous methods you can use to research a crypto asset you're interested in trading. But the primary methods used by investors to evaluate and make informed decisions are fundamental analysis and technical analysis. These methods aim to provide insights into the potential value and future price movements of these assets.

But what is the difference in definition between fundamental analysis and technical analysis?

Fundamental Analysis:

Fundamental analysis involves assessing the intrinsic value of a cryptocurrency or digital asset by analyzing various factors that can influence its price and adoption. It looks at the bigger picture when analyzing the financial status of a crypto asset, the user community, and potential real-world utility.

Fundamental analysis can help you understand whether a digital asset is overpriced or underpriced based on how you view its intrinsic value. In other words, you can evaluate whether an asset will be useful in the future or not, based on your investment goals. For example, Ethereum was designed to support, among other services, decentralized finance (DeFi) applications. In this case, if you believe that DeFi will grow then you might invest in Ethereum as its value is likely to rise in the future.

Key components of fundamental analysis in the context of digital assets investment options include:

i. *Whitepapers and Technology:* Examining the underlying technology, blockchain protocol, consensus mechanism, and the uniqueness of the cryptocurrency's use case.

ii. *Team and Development*: It involves researching the team behind the project, their experience, and their track record in the blockchain and technology space.

iii. *Market Demand and Adoption:* Evaluating the real-world applications and demand for cryptocurrency. This could involve looking at partnerships, collaborations, and the ecosystem it operates in.

iv. *Tokenomics:* Analyzing the supply dynamics, distribution of tokens, inflation rates, and mechanisms that can affect the scarcity and value of the cryptocurrency.

v. *Regulatory Environment:* Considering the legal and regulatory landscape in various jurisdictions, changes in regulations can significantly impact the value and legality of a cryptocurrency.

vi. *Macro-Economic Factors*: Assessing broader economic trends and events that might influence the adoption and value of cryptocurrencies.

vii. *Community and Social Sentiment:* Monitoring online communities, forums, and social media platforms to gauge sentiment and engagement levels among users and investors.

Technical Analysis:

Technical analysis involves examining historical price and trading volume data to make predictions about future price movements. This approach assumes that all relevant information is already reflected in the price, and patterns and trends in price charts can help predict future price directions. By analyzing price and trading volume over time, you can get a sense of how the market sees the asset. The kinds of questions technical analysis asks include: Is the price rising or falling? Are investors putting money in or taking it out? Is it traded widely in the market and large quantities?

Technical analysis focuses on short to medium-term price movements, hence a preferred method of analysis for day traders.

Key components of technical analysis include:

i. Price Patterns: Identifying recurring patterns in price charts, such as triangles, flags, and head-and-shoulders formations, that can indicate potential price trends.

ii. Indicators and Oscillators: Using technical indicators like moving averages, Relative Strength Index (RSI), and MACD (Moving Average Convergence Divergence) to assess market momentum, overbought or oversold conditions, and potential trend reversals.

iii. Support and Resistance Levels: Identifying key price levels where the asset tends to find support (prices stop falling) or resistance (prices stop rising), which can help predict potential price movements.

iv. Volume Analysis: Examining trading volume alongside price movements to determine the strength of trends and potential reversals.

v. Chart Patterns: Recognizing chart patterns like double tops, double bottoms, and ascending/descending triangles that can indicate shifts in market sentiment.

As you can see from the above-listed parameters, technical analysis is more of a numbers-driven strategy. It generally assumes that the market has already done the work of incorporating all the known information via the current price, and the amount of the trading activity, which is found on crypto-data sites like CoinGecko and Nomics.

Similarly, advocates of technical analysis believe that because the current prices reflect market forces like supply and demand, the price of an asset should give you a snapshot of how the public feels about it right now. This is known as market sentiment- an indicator traders use to predict trends that they use to make investment decisions.

Both fundamental analysis and technical analysis are valuable ways of understanding the opportunities and risks of investing in a digital asset. They can help you build a trading strategy and identify when you want to buy or sell a particular digital asset. Unless you have access to a more advanced model and tools that some pro traders use, it's advisable to employ both strategies together to get a fuller view of your trading journey. As such, many investors use a combination of both approaches to make well-rounded investment decisions.

It's important to note that the cryptocurrency market can be highly volatile and influenced by factors unique to the digital asset space. Therefore, conducting thorough research and staying updated with the latest developments is crucial for making informed investment decisions.

- Comparison of different investment approaches, including buy and hold, dollar-cost averaging, and trading

Many investors are looking to figure out the best ways to incorporate digital assets like Bitcoin and other alternative coins into their investment portfolios. This is driven by the fact that digital assets like Bitcoins have so far outperformed the broader stock market. The major drawback of these digital assets is that they are highly speculative assets with unique risks that you must account for during trading. When it comes down to it, you should have a strategy in place to guide your investing moves, just as you do with traditional assets like stocks and bonds. The three common digital assets investment approaches are Buy and Hold, Dollar-Cost Averaging (DCA), and Trading.

Here is the comparison between the three common digital assets:

Strategy	Explained	Advantages	Disadvantages
Buy & Hold	By & Hold involves purchasing a cryptocurrency and holding onto it for an extended period, regardless of short-term price fluctuations.	A relatively simple and less time-consuming strategy. It can be effective for long-term investors who believe in the potential of a particular cryptocurrency.	It exposes investors to the full volatility of the market. If the market crashes, substantial losses can occur. It also requires strong conviction and patience during market downturns.

Dollar-Cost Averaging (DCA)	DCA involves investing a fixed amount of money at regular intervals (daily, weekly, monthly) regardless of the cryptocurrency's price. This leads to buying more when prices are low and less when prices are high.	DCA reduces the impact of market volatility, as it automatically buys more when prices are lower, potentially lowering the average cost per unit. It's a disciplined approach that removes the need to time the market.	While it reduces risk, it might also limit potential gains if the market experiences a strong upward trend. Some opportunities for large gains during market bottoms might be missed.
Trading	Trading involves actively buying and selling cryptocurrencies to profit from short-term price movements. Traders use various techniques such as technical analysis, fundamental analysis, and sentiment analysis to make decisions	If done skillfully, trading can provide quick profits, and there are various strategies to adapt to different market conditions. It's also possible to profit in both rising and falling markets.	Trading requires a deep understanding of the market, technical analysis, and risk management. It's time-intensive and can lead to significant losses if not done properly due to the high volatility of cryptocurrencies. Emotional decision-making and fees can also eat into profits.

Choosing the right approach depends on your investment goals, risk tolerance, time commitment, and market knowledge. As illustrated in the table above, each approach has its own advantages and drawbacks, and there's no one-size-fits-all solution. Some investors might use a combination of these strategies based on their preferences and circumstances. Before making any investment decisions, it's essential to conduct thorough research, consider your financial situation, and perhaps consult with financial professionals.

Unstoppable Domains:

One notable innovation in the digital asset space is Unstoppable Domains, a pioneering solution to the complexity of crypto addresses. Established in 2018 by CEO Matthew Gould, the platform addresses the challenge of user-friendly crypto address interactions. The company's vision is reminiscent of the Domain Name System (DNS) that revolutionized website access by replacing the need to remember IP addresses. Similarly, Unstoppable Domains aims to create an equivalent system for crypto addresses, streamlining the process for users. Unstoppable Domains is the alternative to centralized domains such as Google Domains, Namecheap, IONOS Hosting, iPage, and Network Solutions among others.

Unstoppable Domains has achieved significant success in this endeavor. They have developed a unique domain system that enables users to configure payments for 276 different digital assets under a single domain name. Additionally, these domains can function as fully operational websites, capable of integrating decentralized applications (dApps), due to their blockchain-based hosting. The service's appeal is bolstered by its one-time payment structure without annual renewal fees, making it an enticing tool for crypto enthusiasts and businesses alike.

Security is a paramount concern in the crypto space, and Unstoppable Domains excels in this aspect. Once a domain is claimed, it becomes an immutable entity on the blockchain, inheriting the security features of the underlying blockchain technology. This renders Unstoppable Domains highly secure, as any alteration requires consensus within the blockchain network. Moreover, the censorship-resistant nature of blockchain ensures that domains cannot be blocked by external parties, safeguarding websites from potential takedowns. The platform's purchasing process also maintains security standards and offers the option of enhancing security with two-factor authentication.

The cost of acquiring Unstoppable Domains varies based on two primary factors. Notably, the purchase cost is a one-time expense, eliminating the need for recurring payments. The initial factor is the domain's price, ranging from $20 to over US$1000 depending on factors such as domain type (e.g., .crypto vs. .wallet) and name length, with shorter domains incurring higher costs. Premium domains may command even higher prices, reaching tens of thousands of dollars. The second factor involves the Ethereum gas fee, associated with claiming the domain on the Ethereum blockchain. As these domains are stored on Ethereum, the gas fee, denominated in ETH, is separate from the initial purchase cost. The exact gas fee depends on prevailing ETH prices and network congestion, but obtaining a budget-friendly .crypto domain and completing the claim for under $50 is feasible.

Unstoppable Domains boasts several compelling features that set it apart. The one-time purchase model with no recurring fees stands out against traditional domain ownership practices. Additionally, the censorship-resistant nature of these domains ensures they can only be controlled by their rightful owners, shielding them from arbitrary takedowns. Their blockchain-based hosting affords them greater functionality than conventional domains, enabling users to create websites with embedded dApps through smart contracts. Perhaps the most remarkable feature is the ability to consolidate crypto assets: a single domain can serve as a unified address for receiving 276 different cryptocurrencies. This not only simplifies transactions for users but also enhances the ease of receiving funds for recipients.

However, Unstoppable Domains is not without potential drawbacks. The primary concern revolves around the cost of claiming a domain using Ethereum. For users without existing Ethereum holdings, acquiring the necessary ETH to complete the domain claim might be an extra step. Additionally, some might find the gas fees associated with the Ethereum transaction to be a barrier. Nonetheless, it's essential to note that these fees are a one-time expense and should be evaluated in the context of the long-term benefits and convenience provided by Unstoppable Domains.

Nonetheless, Unstoppable Domain has continued to prove a viable investment destination for many investors with its groundbreaking solutions to simplify interactions with crypto addresses and enable blockchain-based websites. With its secure, censorship-resistant nature, streamlined payment structure, and innovative features, Unstoppable Domains offers a compelling proposition for crypto enthusiasts and businesses looking to enhance their online presence and transaction processes. While the initial Ethereum transaction cost might raise some concerns, the long-term advantages and convenience provided by these domains make them a compelling addition to the evolving landscape of blockchain technology, hence massive investment opportunities for investors looking for a rise in the market value of a digital asset.

Conclusion

The chapter provides a comprehensive roadmap for navigating the intricate world of digital asset investment. It acknowledges the extraordinary opportunities presented by this burgeoning field while advocating for diligent research, adaptability, and the judicious application of diverse strategies to make informed crypto investment choices. With the digital asset realm poised for continued maturation, staying attuned to developments and embracing versatile approaches will be key in harnessing the potential rewards of this evolving financial landscape.

RISKS AND CHALLENGES OF INVESTING IN DIGITAL ASSETS

In an era defined by technological innovation and the relentless pursuit of financial growth, digital assets have emerged as both a disruptive force and a tantalizing opportunity in the world of investment. The rapid rise of cryptocurrencies, blockchain technology, and various digital tokens has sparked the curiosity of seasoned investors and newcomers alike. Yet, within this promising landscape lies a complex web of risks and challenges that demand careful examination and understanding.

Discussion of potential risks and challenges associated with investing in digital assets

As cryptocurrencies, non-fungible tokens (NFTs), and other digital instruments gain traction, they offer unparalleled liquidity, borderless accessibility, and novel methods of value exchange. However, as investors increasingly flock to these alluring prospects, they are met with an intricate web of risks that demand attention.

A central theme of this chapter revolves around the volatility inherent in digital asset markets. Unlike traditional assets, which often display a degree of stability, digital assets are infamous for their extreme price fluctuations. This volatility stems from a variety of factors, including regulatory uncertainties, technological vulnerabilities, market sentiment shifts, and the relatively nascent nature of the assets themselves. The chapter dissects how these factors intertwine, triggering both rapid gains and precipitous losses that can challenge even the most experienced investors.

Moreover, the issue of security takes center stage. The decentralized nature of blockchain technology does provide a robust layer of security, yet digital assets are not impervious to threats. Hacking incidents, phishing attacks, and vulnerabilities in smart contracts have

resulted in substantial financial losses, underscoring the importance of understanding the nuances of digital asset storage and the critical role of cybersecurity measures. Within the security issues is the realm of fraudulent schemes and scams that have proliferated within the digital asset ecosystem. From Ponzi schemes to deceptive initial coin offerings (ICOs), unsuspecting investors are susceptible to falling prey to fraudulent actors who exploit the relative anonymity of the digital landscape. Understanding the hallmarks of such scams becomes paramount for investors to protect their interests.

The regulatory landscape forms another pivotal aspect of the discussion. The absence of a universally standardized regulatory framework has led to a patchwork of differing approaches across jurisdictions. This lack of clarity introduces significant uncertainty for investors, influencing market dynamics and potentially exposing them to legal risks. The chapter evaluates various regulatory stances around the world and their impact on investment decisions.

Explanation of market risks, security risks, and regulatory risks

Market risks

The digital assets market, encompassing cryptocurrencies and other blockchain-based tokens, has garnered significant attention in recent years due to its potential for high returns. However, this market is characterized by extreme volatility, which presents serious risks and challenges to investors. This volatility arises from a combination of factors unique to the digital assets ecosystem, and it can have far-reaching consequences for both individual and institutional investors.

Additionally, the speculative nature of digital asset trading amplifies volatility. Many investors are drawn to the potential for quick and substantial gains, leading to a disproportionate focus on short-term price movements rather than the underlying fundamentals of the assets. This speculative behavior creates a feedback loop where price swings are exacerbated by emotional reactions, contributing to market instability.

Moreover, the lack of intrinsic value in many digital assets complicates their valuation and increases uncertainty. Unlike traditional assets like stocks or bonds that can be analyzed based on earnings, dividends, or interest rates, many digital assets lack clear fundamental metrics. This ambiguity can lead to exaggerated price swings as market sentiment shifts.

For instance, the prices of digital assets went through a roller-coaster year in 2022. The main cause of the market slump was the collapse of FTX, one of the biggest global cryptocurrency exchanges. FTX's financial troubles and its feud with Binance not only triggered a massive sell-off but also drained liquidity from the crypto market.

Binance, the world's largest cryptocurrency platform, had plans to acquire its rival, FTX. However, Binance surprisingly backed out of the deal, pointing to various financial issues and ongoing regulatory investigations involving FTX. This unexpected move by Binance caught crypto investors off guard and sent Bitcoin plummeting to its lowest point in two years, from a record high of $69,000 in November 2021 to below $20,000 in 6 months.[6] These unforeseen developments created a state of turmoil in the cryptocurrency industry. As a result, investors grew increasingly distrustful and skeptical of centralized crypto institutions and regulatory efforts.

For investors, such an occurrence poses several risks and challenges. First and foremost, there is the risk of substantial financial loss. Sudden price drops can wipe out investments, and the unpredictability of the market makes it difficult to time trades effectively. Furthermore, the emotional toll of dealing with extreme volatility can lead to poor decision-making and irrational behavior, compounding potential losses.

The challenges also extend to institutional investors and financial institutions. They may be hesitant to fully engage in the digital assets market due to concerns about their reputation. Additionally, the lack of established risk management tools for digital assets further complicates their integration into traditional investment portfolios.

However, as the market continues to evolve, addressing these issues will be essential for achieving a more stable and mature digital assets ecosystem that can attract broader participation and mitigate the inherent risks.

Security Risks

Investing in digital assets carries with it some significant security risks. These risks stem from the unique nature of digital assets and the decentralized technologies that underpin them.

The risks include:

i. *Cyber Theft and Hacking*: Digital assets are stored in digital wallets, which are vulnerable to hacking and cyber theft. Hackers can exploit vulnerabilities in exchanges, wallets, or users' devices to gain unauthorized access and steal funds. Major breaches have resulted in substantial losses, undermining investor confidence. For example, hackers stole $196 million worth of cryptocurrencies from Bitmart in December 2021, following the successful hacking of the centralized crypto exchange.

ii. *Liquidity Risks*: Some digital assets suffer from limited liquidity, meaning they can't be easily converted to cash without causing significant price slippage. This can hinder investors' ability to exit positions quickly, especially during periods of market stress.

---

6   https://www.thetimes.co.uk/money-mentor/article/is-bitcoin-crash-coming/#:~:text=The%20slump%20in%20November%202022,the%20first%20time%20since%202020.

iii. *Private Key Loss*: Digital asset ownership is tied to private keys—sophisticated cryptographic codes. If a private key is lost, stolen, or forgotten, the associated assets are irretrievably lost. According to a recent study, approximately 20% of the total supply of Bitcoin, worth billions of dollars, is lost due to forgotten passwords or lost wallets. This emphasizes the importance of secure storage practices.

iv. *Phishing and Social Engineering*: Scammers use phishing attacks and social engineering tactics to trick investors into revealing their private keys or transferring assets to fraudulent addresses. This can result in substantial losses for unsuspecting individuals.

v. *Fraudulent ICOs and Projects*: Initial Coin Offerings (ICOs) and token projects often lack proper due diligence and regulatory oversight, making them susceptible to fraud. Investors risk losing funds by investing in projects that fail to deliver promised outcomes or have malicious intent.

vi. *Technological Risks:* Digital assets rely on complex technologies like blockchain. Flaws in these technologies, including smart contracts, can be exploited by malicious actors, leading to financial losses or systemic disruptions.

vii. *Human Error*: Investors themselves can inadvertently expose their assets to risk. Errors like sending funds to incorrect addresses, or falling for scams can lead to irreversible losses.

In summary, while digital assets offer promising investment opportunities, they come with inherent security risks that demand careful consideration, due diligence, and proactive security measures from investors.

Regulatory Risks

Unlike traditional financial markets that are subject to established regulatory frameworks, the digital assets market has for many years operated in a relatively unregulated environment. This absence of oversight can lead to sudden market manipulation, fraudulent schemes, and insider trading, which contribute to rapid price fluctuations. Furthermore, the decentralized and often cross-border nature of cryptocurrencies presents challenges for traditional regulatory frameworks, leading to a complex and evolving landscape. These regulatory uncertainties can have a profound impact on the industry, affecting market dynamics, investor confidence, innovation, and adoption.

Impact of Regulatory Risks:

i. *Market Volatility:* Regulatory developments or announcements can trigger significant price volatility in the cryptocurrency market. Positive regulatory news may lead to price surges, while negative news can result in sharp declines. For instance, when major countries like China or India announced bans or restrictions on cryptocurrencies, the market often experienced significant drops in value.

ii. *Investor Confidence:* Lack of clear regulations or sudden changes in regulatory stances can erode investor confidence. Uncertainty about the legality and treatment of digital assets can deter institutional investors and mainstream adoption.

iii. *Innovation and Development:* Regulatory uncertainty can impede innovation and the development of new projects within the cryptocurrency space. Startups and entrepreneurs may be hesitant to invest time and resources into projects if the regulatory environment is uncertain or hostile.

iv. *Geographical Fragmentation:* Different countries and jurisdictions have taken varying approaches to regulating cryptocurrencies, leading to a fragmented global landscape. This can create challenges for businesses operating across borders and result in a lack of harmonization in regulatory standards.

Digital Assets Affected by Regulatory Issues

Regulatory issues have significantly impacted various digital assets, with even the pioneering cryptocurrency, Bitcoin, not immune to their effects. The following are just a few examples of digital assets that have been adversely affected by regulatory issues:

Bitcoin (BTC): Bitcoin, being the first and most recognizable cryptocurrency, has frequently found its value swayed by regulatory updates. The mere announcements of bans, limitations, or positive regulatory shifts in different nations have triggered substantial fluctuations in its price.

Ethereum (ETH): Ethereum's Ether token serves not only as a digital currency but also fuels decentralized applications (dApps) through its smart contract capabilities. The uncertainty surrounding regulations can cast a shadow on the development and acceptance of these dApps, which in turn affects the valuation of Ether.

Ripple (XRP): Ripple Labs encountered legal action from the U.S. Securities and Exchange Commission (SEC) regarding whether XRP should be categorized as a security. This legal conflict led to a notable drop in XRP's value and brought forth inquiries about the regulatory standing of other cryptocurrencies.

Stablecoins: Stablecoins, exemplified by Tether (USDT) and USD Coin (USDC), are engineered to maintain a stable worth by pegging them to traditional assets like the U.S. dollar. Apprehensions over the reserves supporting these stablecoins or their potential repercussions on monetary systems have spurred variations in their usage and valuation.

Privacy Coins: Cryptocurrencies like Monero (XMR) and Zcash (ZEC) prioritize augmented privacy features, raising regulators' concerns about their potential misuse of illicit activities. Actions taken by regulators to curtail or limit privacy coins can bring about fluctuations in their market value.

Initial Coin Offerings (ICOs): Although Initial Coin Offerings have waned in popularity due to regulatory worries, they played a pivotal role in procuring funds for numerous blockchain projects. Regulatory interventions against ICOs or their classification as securities have impacted investor sentiment, thereby contributing to instability within the market.

In summary, regulatory risks wield a momentous influence in molding the cryptocurrency and digital asset sphere. The ever-evolving regulatory landscape will persistently shape market dynamics and chart the course for the broader blockchain ecosystem. Therefore, as an investor, it is necessary to vigilantly track regulatory advancements to help you adapt your trading strategies accordingly.

Strategies for Mitigating Digital Assets Investment Risks

As the world becomes increasingly digital, digital assets have emerged as a new frontier for investment. However, with great potential comes significant risks. Mitigating these risks is crucial to ensure successful digital asset investments. Strategies to navigate these challenges encompass careful research, diversification, regulatory compliance, secure storage, and risk management.

i.   Thorough Research: In the digital asset space, thorough research is fundamental. As an investor, you should understand the technology, use cases, and market dynamics of the specific digital assets they intend to invest in. This includes studying whitepapers, assessing development teams, and staying updated on industry trends. A solid understanding can help you distinguish between promising projects and potential scams, reducing the risk of fraudulent investments.

ii. Diversification: Diversifying a digital asset portfolio is a strategy that can help mitigate risks. Rather than putting all resources into a single asset, spreading investments across different types of digital assets can lower the impact of a poor-performing asset on the overall portfolio. Diversification enables exposure to various projects with different risk profiles, potentially leading to more stable and sustainable returns.

iii. Regulatory Compliance: Navigating the regulatory landscape is essential to avoid legal complications. Digital assets often fall under different regulatory frameworks globally. Ensuring compliance with local regulations can reduce the risk of legal actions that could jeopardize investments. Staying informed about evolving regulations and

iv. Secure Storage: Digital assets, such as cryptocurrencies, are susceptible to cyberattacks due to their digital nature. Implementing robust security measures for storage is paramount. This includes using hardware wallets, secure software wallets, and employing best practices like two-factor authentication. By safeguarding private keys and employing encryption, you can significantly reduce the risk of theft or unauthorized access to their assets.

v. Risk Management: Implementing effective risk management strategies is vital to navigating the volatile nature of digital asset markets. Setting clear investment goals, defining risk tolerance, and adhering to a well-thought-out exit strategy can help prevent emotional decision-making during market fluctuations. You should avoid making impulsive decisions driven by fear or greed and instead, base your actions on a predetermined plan.

vi. Due Diligence: Performing due diligence on platforms and exchanges is critical before conducting transactions. Investors should assess the security features, reputation, and regulatory compliance of the platforms they intend to use. Choosing reputable exchanges can reduce the risk of encountering fraudulent schemes or hacking incidents that may compromise investments.

vii. Long-Term Perspective: Investing in digital assets with a long-term perspective can help mitigate the risks associated with short-term price volatility. While digital asset markets are known for their rapid price fluctuations, adopting a patient approach can allow you to weather market turbulence and capture the potential value of innovative projects over time.

viii. Continuous Learning: The digital asset landscape is constantly evolving, with new technologies and investment opportunities arising regularly. Engaging in continuous learning through online communities, forums, and educational resources can help you stay up-to-date with industry developments, enabling you to make informed decisions based on the latest information.

ix. Monitoring and Adaptation: Regularly monitoring the performance of investments and adjusting strategies as needed is crucial. Market conditions can change rapidly, and staying attuned to these changes allows you to adapt your portfolios accordingly. Being proactive rather than reactive can help mitigate risks and capitalize on emerging opportunities.

x. Professional Advice: If you're new to the digital asset space, seeking advice from professionals with experience in blockchain technology and investment can be beneficial. Financial advisors or consultants with expertise in digital assets can provide valuable insights and guide you through the complexities of the market.

Conclusion

While digital assets offer enticing opportunities, they are fraught with complexities. The chapter emphasizes the volatility of digital asset markets, driven by factors like regulatory uncertainties, technology vulnerabilities, and market sentiment shifts. Security risks are a concern due to cyber theft, hacking, private key loss, phishing, and technological flaws. Regulatory risks arise from the absence of standardized frameworks, impacting market dynamics and investor confidence. To be a successful digital assets investor, it is important to ensure thorough research, diversification, regulatory compliance, secure storage, risk management, due diligence, a long-term perspective, continuous learning, monitoring, and seeking professional advice can significantly mitigate these risks. By adopting a cautious and informed approach, investors can increase their chances of success in the dynamic world of digital asset investments.

TAXATION AND REGULATION

Overview of taxation and regulation of digital assets

Over the last decade, the rapid growth of digital assets has seen advocates envision a new era of financial liberation, with trust shifting from traditional institutions to secure decentralized ledgers, leading to cost reductions in transactions. There has never been a time when cryptocurrencies herald decentralized finance innovations, revolutionizing the financial system. Critics, however, label crypto markets as the "Wild West," citing criminal activities, uninformed investors, and massive price fluctuations. Once at $3 trillion in 2021, the market value has plummeted to just about $1 trillion, marked by instances like the collapse of FTX, an exchange platform with its own cryptocurrency.

The environmental and intrinsic value concerns also fuel debate. Detractors argue that crypto creation damages the environment and lacks inherent value, highlighting the rise of "green cryptocurrencies" and comparing fiat currencies' valuelessness. Proponents counter the speed, ease, and support crypto offers, exemplified by its aid to Ukraine and the promise of ongoing innovation benefits.

For regulators, the challenge is striking a balance between fostering innovation and ensuring financial stability and investor protection. Tax authorities grapple with incorporating crypto assets into functioning tax systems. Regardless of crypto's future trajectory, addressing it within the tax framework remains crucial.

Taxation and crypto assets raise issues of potential tax evasion, particularly among the wealthy. Some individuals have accumulated substantial wealth through crypto, prompting scrutiny of their tax liabilities. The paper recognizes the limited research and empirical evidence in this complex domain and emphasizes the technical difficulties policymakers face.

The section focuses on the tax implications of crypto assets' rise. It underscores that tax systems were not designed for non-national currency trades, exacerbated by the anonymity of crypto transactions that echoes cash use. This raises concerns about capital income and sales taxation. Despite challenges in the nascent field, we acknowledge the potential for distributed ledger and smart contract technologies to enhance tax administration based on various tax laws amidst regulatory challenges.

Explanation of different tax laws and regulations in various countries

The intricate relationship between cryptocurrencies and tax design has become a pivotal consideration for policymakers worldwide. The complexities of how cryptocurrencies are created, exchanged, and utilized raise crucial questions about income taxation, value-added tax (VAT), and sales taxes. The global landscape of cryptocurrency taxation varies widely among countries, with ongoing changes and clarifications shaping the regulatory environment.

A fundamental principle guiding the tax treatment of cryptocurrencies is that of neutrality, aiming to treat them similarly to traditional financial instruments, except for considerations of externalities. This principle applies to both income taxation and VAT/sales taxes, to ensure fairness and consistency across different types of assets.

A. Income Taxation

The multifaceted nature of cryptocurrencies as both investment assets and mediums of exchange poses a challenge when classifying them for income tax purposes. Two primary classifications have emerged: treating digital assets as property (akin to stocks or bonds) or as foreign currency. The distinction between these classifications holds significant taxation implications. For instance, classifying cryptocurrencies as property often subjects them to capital gains tax. However, specific details such as loss ring-fencing, exempt amounts, and variable tax rates based on holding periods can greatly impact the tax outcome.

In the United States, cryptocurrencies are treated as property, necessitating the reporting of capital gains on all transactions. A lower tax rate, similar to that of ordinary income tax, applies if the assets are held for over a year. Contrastingly, characterizing cryptocurrencies as currency would result in gains being taxed as ordinary income, but only on amounts exceeding a particular threshold. Similar complexities arise globally, with treating cryptocurrencies as property requiring meticulous gain/loss calculations for each transaction. This intricate process can pose significant burdens for small users, hindering the widespread adoption of cryptocurrencies for everyday transactions.

An intriguing alternative is an analogy drawn between digital asset holdings and gambling. Some suggest taxing digital asset gains like gambling winnings, which would have implications for income, VAT, and sales taxes. However, the validity of this analogy remains uncertain, as research indicates varying reasons for digital asset holdings.

Currently, the prevailing approach globally is to treat cryptocurrencies as property for income tax purposes, subjecting them to corresponding capital gains tax rules. However, individual countries diverge in their implementations. Several nations, including those in Europe, Malaysia, and Singapore, exempt or tax capital gains from financial assets differently based on holding periods. Portugal initially exempted gains on crypto holdings to promote a crypto-friendly environment, while El Salvador continues to provide an outright exemption.

India presents a distinctive case, with a unique tax regime targeting gains and trading income from "virtual digital assets" (VDAs), encompassing cryptocurrencies and similar tokens. This regime includes a 30% tax on such gains and a 1% surcharge on VDA transfers.

B. VAT and Sales Taxation

The application of VAT and sales taxes to cryptocurrency transactions aligns with the broader tax principles applied to barter transactions. Many countries explicitly exempt cryptocurrency-for-fiat transactions from VAT, recognizing cryptocurrencies as a form of "consideration" within the framework of these taxes. Notably, the European Union's Court of Justice ruled in 2015 that VAT should not apply to cryptocurrency-for-fiat transactions.

The taxation of fees and newly created cryptocurrencies received by miners presents another aspect of VAT and sales tax policy. While there is no inherent reason to exempt these transactions from VAT, many countries, in practice, exempt financial service fees from VAT. This divergence can result in over-taxation for business cryptocurrency use and under-taxation for personal use.

Externalities and Corrective Taxation

The use of cryptocurrencies carries potential externalities that challenge traditional regulatory frameworks. Beyond conventional concerns about financial stability, consumer protection, and criminal activity, cryptocurrencies introduce unique challenges tied directly to their usage.

For instance, the analogy between cryptocurrency holdings and gambling suggests issues of self-control that could justify corrective taxation. The widespread adoption of cryptocurrencies might also disrupt macroeconomic management tools, necessitating corrective measures to counter these risks. These potential risks have prompted discussions about a cryptocurrency transactions tax, similar to financial transaction taxes, to manage these challenges. However, implementing such a tax faces practical challenges, potentially driving transactions underground or offshore.

Environmental concerns constitute a compelling case for corrective taxation. The energy-intensive nature of proof-of-work consensus mechanisms, such as Bitcoin's, contributes to significant carbon emissions. Some governments have proposed or implemented taxes targeting miners' electricity usage, aiming to internalize the environmental costs. The Biden administration and Kazakhstan have introduced such taxes, but their effectiveness and differentiation based on carbon intensity are areas of ongoing debate.

Ultimately, the evolving landscape of cryptocurrency taxation illustrates the intricate balance between innovation, fairness, and environmental responsibility. Countries continue to grapple with designing tax frameworks that account for the unique characteristics of cryptocurrencies while addressing potential externalities and fostering a stable economic environment.

Discussion of regulatory challenges facing the cryptocurrency market

Since their inception, digital assets have raised significant concerns about their potential for enabling criminal activities due to their inherent anonymity. Criminal exploitation of cryptocurrencies is undeniably widespread, as evidenced by prominent seizures like the staggering USD 3.6 billion Bitcoin confiscation in February 2022. This criminal usage extends to traditional offenses such as money laundering, drug trade, and terrorism financing, as well as emerging digital crimes like online fraud and ransomware attacks. Alongside these concerns, the connection between Bitcoin adoption and indicators of institutional quality and corruption implies a shadowy aspect of the crypto ecosystem.

Tax evasion, while also associated with digital assets, often takes a back seat in discussions. Yet, it is vital to explore both the extent of crypto's role in criminal activities and its potential as a tool for evading taxes. This analysis dives into these two dimensions, shedding light on the intricate relationship between crypto, crime, and taxes.

A. *Digital Assets and Crime*

The utilization of cryptocurrencies in serious criminal activities provides more clarity compared to their role in tax evasion. Thanks to the blockchain's transparent record of all transactions, researchers have been able to gather insights into the extent of hardcore criminal involvement.

Foley et al. (2019) examine over 600 million blockchain transactions spanning from 2009 to April 2017.[7] They identify addresses linked to seizures and darknet trading and

7   Foley, S., Jonathan, K., and Putnin, š, T. (2019). "Sex, Drugs, and Bitcoin: How Much Illegal Activity Is Financed through Cryptocurrencies?" *Review of Financial Studies*, 32, 1798–1853. https://doi.org/10.1093/rfs/hhz015

estimate a broader group engaging in illegal activities. Their study concludes that around 25 percent of Bitcoin users in 2017 were involved in criminal endeavors, accounting for a considerable portion of transactions and holding a substantial share of Bitcoins. However, contrasting estimates by Chainalysis and Makarov-Schoar point to a much smaller scale of illegal activities facilitated by cryptocurrencies.

While discrepancies exist in these estimates, consensus emerges on the declining relative importance of crypto-enabled crime. Traditional financing methods, including cash, still dominate criminal activities. Furthermore, the digital asset landscape continues to evolve towards enhanced anonymity, with cryptocurrencies like Monero prioritizing privacy through non-disclosure of transaction details.

B. *The Dynamics of Tax Evasions*

Considering that the proceeds from criminal activities are typically taxable, evaluations of crypto-enabled crime inherently encompass a degree of tax evasion. However, in the context of serious crimes, tax evasion is often a secondary outcome. Criminals focus on laundering money to legitimize illegal gains, potentially leading to some form of taxation.

From a tax perspective, three critical questions emerge. Firstly, the incentives driving crypto's use for evading taxes on lawful transactions. Secondly, the extent to which cryptocurrencies contribute to tax evasion. Lastly, the proper payment of taxes related to crypto assets themselves. Unfortunately, solid insights into these inquiries are scarce.

Digital assets' impact on tax evasion aligns with classic considerations outlined in Allingham and Sandmo (1972). This involves weighing the potential tax savings against the risks of detection, wherein crypto's anonymity amplifies its allure as an evasion tool. Transaction costs also factor in, although the balance between crypto and cash remains intricate. High price volatility and risks of fraud associated with cryptocurrencies could discourage evasion.

Quantifying the extent of crypto-enabled tax evasion remains challenging. Occasional news stories about evaded taxes using digital assets provide anecdotal evidence, but there's a dearth of concrete data. Efforts in India and the UK to combat VAT fraud through crypto highlight the issue's complexity.

C. *Tax Compliance*

Gauging tax compliance regarding cryptocurrencies presents its own challenges. In the US, a mere one percent of returns in 2020 reported crypto sales, despite survey evidence suggesting higher crypto ownership rates. Similar patterns emerge in the UK, where some owners are aware of tax obligations, but a complete understanding remains elusive. While there are indications of compliance, they're far from comprehensive.

A notable attempt to assess compliance is the examination of tax loss harvesting by crypto owners, where losses are realized and then repurchased to exploit tax benefits. Studies suggest these practices increase following IRS statements about crypto taxation, revealing a mix of compliance and non-compliance tendencies.

The current understanding of the potential revenue implications, whether from collection or evasion, remains rather unclear. Among the efforts to shed light on this, Thiemann's research in 2021 stands out. By utilizing Bitcoin transaction data provided by Chainalysis and making probabilistic connections to users' countries based on web traffic patterns and other indicators like time zone disparities, Thiemann estimated the capital gains accrued and realized by residents of the European Union (EU).[8] While the precise figures for capital gains tax payment on these transactions remain elusive, this approach allows for a rough estimation of the theoretically owed taxes—essentially serving as an upper limit for potential tax evasion. According to these estimates, the evaded tax amount for 2020 is approximately EUR 850–900 million.

Scaling this against the backdrop of the broader EU personal capital gains tax revenues, which some countries do not fully disclose, is somewhat challenging. However, Thiemann's research suggests this might represent about 0.3 percent of total property tax revenue in the EU. It's worth noting that this amount also pales in comparison to the capital gains tax revenue in the UK alone (which wasn't part of the sample), estimated to be around EUR 12 billion.

Given the considerable lack of knowledge in this realm, even rudimentary calculations can be informative. One such approach is treating cryptocurrencies as investment assets and applying assumed rates of return and taxation. Assuming a total crypto market capitalization of USD 1 trillion (for context, global "hidden wealth" estimates hover around USD 7 trillion), a 5 percent return rate, and a 20 percent tax rate, this implies a total tax liability of USD 10 billion. For a peak market valuation of USD 2.6 trillion (November 2021), this surges to an annual USD 26 billion.

While these figures might seem modest on the global stage—the latter being about 1 percent of worldwide corporate income tax revenue—they could still be substantial given the inherent volatility of cryptocurrencies. Reflecting on the past two years underscores the significant revenue swings. Crypto assets' market capitalization soared from USD 752 billion to USD 2.368 trillion in 2021, only to plummet to USD 836 billion in 2022. Assuming a 20 percent tax rate, these swings could have generated hefty tax revenue of USD 323 billion in 2021 and USD 100 billion even in 2022, considering one-third of the gains were realized.

---

8   Thiemann, A. (2021). "Cryptocurrencies: An Empirical View from a Tax Perspective", JRC Working Papers on Taxation and Structural Reforms No 12/2021. https://joint-research-centre.ec.europa.eu/system/files/2021-08/jrc126109.pdf

Considering the concentration of holdings, taxing gains (and offsetting losses) for major holders would yield sizable revenue. In 2021, the implied tax on realized gains for the top 116 addresses could be around USD 17 billion, or around USD 1.4 billion in a more stable scenario.

Another approach might be applying a financial transactions tax to cryptocurrencies, akin to what's proposed for securities trading. With a 0.1 percent rate, this could generate USD 15.8 billion in revenue for crypto transactions totaling USD 15.8 trillion in 2021.

Alternatively, focusing on cryptocurrency's use as a means of payment presents challenges due to differing taxation for various types of transactions. Nonetheless, even with generous assumptions, substantial revenue could be in jeopardy. If all crypto transactions were treated as part of a VAT chain, with final sales constituting 5 percent by value, and a 15 percent VAT rate, potential revenue loss could reach USD 118.5 billion.

These calculations are overly simplified and laden with assumptions. Furthermore, they don't indicate the extent of tax evasion, given that some of this revenue is likely already being collected. A US Joint Committee on Taxation estimate (2021) suggests new crypto reporting requirements could generate USD 1.5 billion in the first year, increasing to USD 4.6 billion in 2031. These figures represent around 1 percent of total individual capital gains tax revenue in 2020.

From these findings, several insights emerge. First, global revenue at stake could range from tens of billions to potentially even higher figures if cryptocurrencies flourish. Second, the recoverable portion is uncertain, particularly considering the difficulty in detecting evasion due to semi-anonymous transactions. Third, a substantial portion of this revenue pertains to substantial cryptocurrency holders. Lastly, the use of cryptocurrencies for legal transactions could have greater implications in revenue terms, particularly in relation to VAT and sales taxes. While much tax-related attention has focused on crypto's income tax aspects, VAT and sales taxes might present the most significant challenges.

In summary, digital assets' potential to facilitate crime and tax evasion is intertwined with their attributes, technological advancements, and evolving regulatory responses. As the digital assets landscape continues to evolve, policymakers, regulators, and researchers must collaborate to navigate these complex dimensions, ensuring a balance between innovation and societal well-being.

BLOCKCHAIN APPLICATIONS AND USE CASES

In this chapter, we dive deeper into the diverse applications and use cases of blockchain technology.

Overview of Blockchain Applications and Use Cases in Various Industries

Originally conceived to support cryptocurrencies, blockchain technology has now gained widespread recognition for its potential to revolutionize various sectors. Projections indicate substantial growth in global spending on blockchain, with an estimated reach of nearly $19 billion by 2024, demonstrating a remarkable compound annual growth rate of 46.4% over five years.

While Bitcoin and other cryptocurrencies have garnered substantial attention, the spotlight is systematically shifting to the blockchain itself, the underlying distributed ledger technology (DLT) powering these digital currencies.

At its core, blockchain technology is fairly straightforward. It functions as a shared database where entries require validation from peer-to-peer networks and encryption.

An effective analogy is viewing it as a highly secure and verified collaborative Google Document. Each entry in this ledger builds upon logical relationships with its predecessors, gaining consensus from the entire network.

Yet, the potential of blockchain surpasses its role as Bitcoin's foundation. Here, we present emerging applications spanning finance, business, government, and beyond.

In the financial services industry, cryptocurrencies harnessed on blockchain have revolutionized cross-border transactions with their swift and cost-effective nature, unsettling traditional remittance systems. Smart contracts, automated and tamper-resistant agreements on the blockchain, have streamlined transactions and reduced the need for intermediaries, curbing fraud risks. Moreover, blockchain has bolstered transparency in auditing and regulatory compliance, augmenting accountability within financial institutions.

Supply chain management has been reshaped by blockchain's capacity to forge an immutable and transparent ledger. Real-time tracking of goods has been enabled, mitigating counterfeiting and ensuring authenticity. By establishing an unchangeable record, stakeholders can trace product origins, nurturing ethical sourcing and sustainability endeavors. Notably, Walmart and IBM's Food Trust initiative showcases how blockchain verifies the provenance of food items.

In healthcare and pharmaceuticals, where safeguarding patient data and ensuring interoperability is pivotal, blockchain offers a decentralized and secure avenue for medical record management. Patients gain control over their data, while authorized entities access it when necessary. Blockchain's applications extend to battling counterfeit drugs, managing clinical trial data, and enhancing drug traceability.

The real estate domain, grappling with title fraud and intricate ownership transfers, has benefited from blockchain's streamlined property transactions. Secure and verifiable records of ownership and transaction history have rendered intermediaries redundant, minimizing fraud risk and paperwork.

Blockchain's transparency and tamper-proof attributes hold promise for secure and credible voting systems. Governments can ensure accurate vote tabulation and protect votes against manipulation, fortifying democratic processes and public trust.

Intellectual property and copyright protection in the digital age have been fortified by blockchain's capability to confirm ownership and provenance of creative works. Smart contracts enforce rightful compensation and deter unauthorized use.

The energy sector stands to be revolutionized by blockchain, enabling peer-to-peer energy trading and lessening dependence on centralized providers. Individuals can generate, store, and sell energy within microgrids, promoting sustainable and decentralized energy production.

Logistics and transportation have embraced blockchain's transparency and immutability to track goods through complex supply chains, curbing disputes and delays.

Discussion of the potential for blockchain to disrupt traditional industries

Blockchain technology has the potential to disrupt a wide range of traditional industries by introducing new levels of transparency, security, efficiency, and decentralization. Its core features, including immutability, distributed ledger, and smart contracts, can bring about transformative changes in various sectors. Here's a discussion of how blockchain could disrupt some traditional industries:

1. Finance and Banking:

One of the earliest and most well-known applications of blockchain is in the financial sector.

At its core, blockchain offers a decentralized and secure system for recording transactions and managing digital assets. This decentralized nature eliminates the need for intermediaries like banks, significantly reducing transaction costs and increasing efficiency. Smart contracts, self-executing agreements embedded within the blockchain, automate complex processes, further streamlining operations. The transparency and immutability of blockchain ledgers enhance trust among participants, reducing the risk of fraud and errors.

In terms of cross-border payments and remittances, blockchain's real-time processing and borderless nature enable swift and cost-effective transactions. Moreover, blockchain enables financial inclusion by granting access to services for the unbanked population through digital identities and decentralized lending platforms. However, challenges such as scalability, regulatory frameworks, and energy consumption need to be addressed for full-scale adoption. Nonetheless, the financial sector is being reshaped by blockchain's potential to enhance security, transparency, and efficiency while fostering new avenues for innovation and global economic connectivity.

2. Supply Chain Management:

Blockchain can revolutionize supply chains by providing end-to-end traceability and transparency. Every step of a product's journey can be recorded on the blockchain, ensuring authenticity, reducing fraud, and enabling quick recalls if needed.

Blockchain technology holds the transformative potential to reshape the supply chain sector by introducing unprecedented transparency, security, and efficiency to its historically intricate and opaque processes. Essentially a decentralized and distributed digital ledger, blockchain ensures secure and immutable recording of transactions. In the context of supply chains, this implies comprehensive monitoring of a product's journey on the blockchain, encompassing everything from raw material acquisition to manufacturing, distribution, and retailing.

Notably, one of the most tangible advantages of blockchain in supply chain management lies in its efficiency gains. The manual, paper-driven record-keeping and verification processes of the past can be supplanted with automated and digitized workflows. This minimizes errors, diminishes delays, and optimizes inventory management. Furthermore, the real-time tracking of goods becomes attainable, granting stakeholders precise insights into product location and status, ultimately trimming lead times and enhancing predictive analytics.

3. Healthcare:

Healthcare is one of the earliest beneficiaries of blockchain technology. The technology has significantly impacted the Healthcare industry by enhancing data security, interoperability, and transparency. By providing a tamper-proof and decentralized system for storing and sharing medical records and sensitive patient information, blockchain mitigates privacy concerns and reduces the risk of data breaches. It also enables seamless sharing of patient data among different healthcare providers, improving care coordination and patient outcomes. Smart contracts and supply chain tracking on the blockchain streamline processes such as drug traceability and clinical trial management, ensuring greater accountability and efficiency. Overall, blockchain's integration in healthcare fosters trust among stakeholders, minimizes administrative burdens, and fosters innovation in data management and patient care.

4. Real Estate:

Blockchain technology has emerged as a revolutionary solution with the potential to streamline complex processes, and one such arena where it can make a significant impact is in property transactions. Traditionally, property transactions involve convoluted procedures, numerous intermediaries, and substantial paperwork, leading to inefficiencies and delays. However, blockchain presents an innovative approach that can simplify this entire process.

Blockchain operates as a decentralized and tamper-proof digital ledger. In the context of property transactions, it can create an immutable record of ownership, providing transparency and security. This means that every change in ownership or property details is recorded in a way that cannot be altered without consensus from the network, mitigating fraudulent activities and disputes.

Moreover, the integration of smart contracts further enhances the potential of blockchain in property transactions. Smart contracts are self-executing agreements with predefined rules. By automating tasks and workflows, they can streamline the buying, selling, and transferring of property titles. This not only reduces human error but also eliminates the need for intermediaries such as title companies. As a result, transaction times are significantly reduced, costs are lowered, and the entire process becomes more accessible and efficient.

5. Voting Systems:

Blockchain technology can enhance the voting process by providing a secure, transparent, and tamper-resistant platform for recording and verifying votes. Through its decentralized nature, each vote can be cryptographically recorded as a unique transaction on the blockchain, ensuring immutability and preventing unauthorized alterations. This enhances voter trust and minimizes the risk of fraud, as the entire voting history is visible and verifiable by all participants. Additionally, blockchain can facilitate real-time updates, streamline voter registration, and enable remote voting, thereby increasing accessibility and participation. However, challenges such as identity verification and scalability must be carefully addressed to fully realize the potential of blockchain in improving the integrity and efficiency of voting systems.

6. Intellectual Property and Copyright:

Blockchain technology can enhance intellectual property and copyright management by providing a transparent, immutable, and decentralized system for tracking ownership, usage, and transactions of creative works. Through smart contracts and digital tokens, blockchain can automate licensing agreements, ensuring proper compensation for creators and rights holders while enabling seamless micropayments for content usage. This would reduce disputes, streamline licensing processes, and prevent unauthorized use of copyrighted materials. Furthermore, the tamper-resistant nature of blockchain ensures the authenticity of original works, making it easier to prove ownership and strengthen the enforcement of copyright claims. Overall, blockchain's attributes of transparency, security, and automation can revolutionize how intellectual property and copyrights are managed and protected.

7. Energy and Utilities:

Blockchain technology has found significant application in the Energy and Utilities sector. By providing a secure and transparent decentralized ledger, blockchain facilitates efficient management of energy transactions, grid operations, and supply chain processes. It enables peer-to-peer energy trading, allowing consumers to directly buy and sell excess energy, promoting renewable energy integration. Smart contracts on the blockchain automate and enforce agreements, reducing administrative costs and minimizing disputes. Additionally, blockchain enhances traceability and accountability in the utility sector by tracking the origin and movement of resources, improving efficiency, and reducing fraud. Overall, blockchain's immutability and consensus mechanisms hold promise for revolutionizing energy and utilities through increased efficiency, transparency, and decentralized control.

8. Insurance:

Insurance is one of the biggest beneficiaries of the blockchain technology. The technology is being increasingly applied in the insurance industry as a secure and transparent way to streamline processes, enhance trust, and reduce fraud. Through its decentralized and immutable nature, blockchain enables insurers to create tamper-proof records of policyholder information, claims, and transactions, ensuring data integrity and minimizing the risk of manipulation. Smart contracts on the blockchain automate claims processing, enabling faster and more accurate payouts based on predefined conditions. This technology fosters collaboration among insurers, reinsurers, and other stakeholders by providing real-time access to shared data, ultimately leading to improved efficiency, cost reduction, and a more trustworthy insurance ecosystem.

9. Logistics and Shipping:

Blockchain technology finds valuable applications in the logistics industry by providing a transparent and immutable digital ledger for tracking and verifying the movement of goods across the supply chain. Through smart contracts and decentralized consensus mechanisms, blockchain ensures secure and real-time recording of transactions, enhancing traceability, reducing fraud, and minimizing disputes among various stakeholders. This technology streamlines documentation, expedites customs processes, and fosters trust among participants, ultimately optimizing logistics operations and fostering greater efficiency in the industry.

10. Education:

Blockchain can offer secure and verifiable credentials, certificates, and degrees, eliminating the need for manual verification processes. This can enhance the credibility of educational institutions and reduce fraudulent claims.

Through its decentralized and immutable ledger, blockchain technology can establish a tamper-proof system for recording and sharing certificates, degrees, and achievements, preventing fraud and enhancing the value of educational qualifications. This fosters a more efficient and trustworthy credential verification process, enables lifelong learning tracking, and facilitates seamless transfer of credits between institutions, ultimately revolutionizing how education records are managed and authenticated.

While the potential for disruption is significant, several challenges must be addressed for widespread adoption. These include regulatory concerns, scalability issues, energy consumption (in the case of certain blockchain networks), interoperability, and the need for education about the technology. Moreover, transitioning from traditional systems to blockchain-based systems requires careful planning and collaboration among stakeholders.

Analyzing Companies utilizing blockchain and their potential for growth

The potential of blockchain technology is no longer a secret confined to the startup industry. It has now made significant strides within Wall Street, finding adoption among prominent tech industry leaders. These ventures are proving to be lucrative investments for shareholders. Here are a few examples of publicly traded companies utilizing blockchain technology, listed on the NASDAQ or New York Stock Exchange:

1. *Walmart*

Walmart is an exemplary use of blockchain for product tracking.

In the realm of multinational corporations leading the way in blockchain integration, retail giant Walmart stands out. The company has harnessed the power of digital ledger technology to elevate its data tracking and management processes within its daily operations. Notably, Walmart has teamed up with IBM, showcasing an exemplary instance of blockchain application in monitoring the journey of meat and poultry items across its stores.

Additionally, Walmart has successfully implemented a comprehensive blockchain system that enables the traceability of information from the initial producer, through intermediaries like brokers and distributors, all the way to the retailer. Thanks to the seamless integration of blockchain technology, both Walmart's employees and consumers can now effortlessly trace products back to their origins.

2. *NVIDIA:*

Known for its innovation in intensive hardware and diverse tech solutions, NVIDIA is also a pioneer in creating crypto chip mining processors (CMPs) for computers. These CMPs enable more GPUs to be controlled by a single CPU, significantly enhancing the efficiency of cryptocurrency mining, particularly for Bitcoin.

3. *Coinbase:*

Operating one of the most widely used crypto exchange platforms, Coinbase serves over 100 million users who can trade and store assets ranging from cryptocurrencies to NFTs. The platform also provides access to crypto wallets, a dedicated Coinbase debit card, and a crypto rewards system. Since going public in 2021, Coinbase has established itself as a consistent contender in the cryptocurrency stock landscape.

4. *PayPal:*

Renowned for its rapid cross-border money transfers for users and businesses globally, PayPal additionally facilitates the purchase, storage, and exchange of cryptocurrencies such as Bitcoin, Bitcoin Cash, Ethereum, and Litecoin. With a user base exceeding 400 million worldwide, PayPal stands as a popular choice for money transfer services.

5. *Advanced Micro Devices (AMD):*

A leader in creating computer hardware and core technologies for data centers, high-performance computing, and gaming, AMD's Blockchain Compute systems unite GPU and CPU hardware to empower secure and optimized blockchain transactions. AMD has also collaborated with other blockchain companies to establish blockchain gaming and rendering platforms.

6. *IBM:*

Beyond aiding businesses in integrating blockchain into their operations, IBM hosts its own blockchain platform and open-source framework called Hyperledger Fabric. This technology has effectively addressed challenges in supply chain management, credential security, and digital asset administration. Over 120,000 organizations contribute to the Hyperledger Fabric project.

7. *Microsoft Azure:*

Through its partnership with ConsenSys, Microsoft's Azure platform offers the Quorum Blockchain Service. This service plays a crucial role in implementing blockchain across various sectors. It provides a managed environment for developing and scaling enterprise blockchain applications and smart contracts in the cloud, utilized by companies like Bosch and Prescryptive Health.

8. *Intel:*

Developed in collaboration with the Linux Foundation, IBM, and SAP, Intel's Hyperledger Sawtooth network is an enterprise-grade blockchain platform tailored for creating applications and smart contracts. The platform emphasizes data protection, open-sourced data collection, and an exceedingly secure ledger. Intel also distributes the Intel Blockscale ASIC, capable of operating at a rate of 580 gigahashes per second for proof-of-work networks.

9. *Block:*

Serving as the parent company for payment platforms and cryptocurrency-related services like Square, Cash App, Spiral, TBD, and Afterpay, Block focuses on enhancing mobile payment accessibility for users and small businesses, alongside crypto banking support. The company has also expanded its reach into media and entertainment with platforms like Weebly and Tidal.

10. *Marathon Digital Holdings:*

With an operational data center housing over 2,000 ASIC Bitcoin miners, Marathon Digital Holdings specializes exclusively in crypto mining and the generation of digital assets. The company's primary objective is to contribute to the development and security of the Bitcoin ecosystem while streamlining corporate expenses and increasing accessibility for investors.

Conclusion

The application of blockchain technology across various industries and use cases has demonstrated its transformative potential in enhancing transparency, security, efficiency, and accountability. Across sectors such as finance, supply chain, healthcare, and more, blockchain has showcased its ability to streamline processes, reduce fraud, and enable new business models.

In the financial industry, blockchain's decentralized nature has led to the creation of cryptocurrencies and decentralized finance (DeFi) platforms, revolutionizing how transactions and financial services are conducted. Supply chain management has seen significant improvements as blockchain ensures the immutability of records, enabling better traceability, reducing counterfeiting, and enhancing consumer trust. In healthcare, blockchain's secure data-sharing capabilities offer solutions for interoperability challenges, allowing for more efficient patient care and data management while maintaining data privacy.

Moreover, smart contracts have automated agreement execution, eliminating intermediaries and reducing costs in various industries. Voting systems have become more secure and transparent, fostering trust in democratic processes. Intellectual property protection and royalty distribution have also been streamlined using blockchain's traceable ledger.

However, challenges such as scalability, energy consumption, regulatory uncertainty, and interoperability still need to be addressed for broader blockchain adoption. As technology continues to evolve, collaboration between industries, governments, and technologists will be crucial in realizing its full potential and addressing these challenges.

In essence, the diverse applications of blockchain highlight its capacity to reshape traditional processes, reimagine business models, and foster a new era of decentralized, secure, and efficient operations across a multitude of sectors. As industries continue to explore and integrate blockchain solutions, its impact is poised to be both lasting and transformative, ushering in a new wave of innovation and possibilities.

FUTURE OF BLOCKCHAIN AND DIGITAL ASSETS

Analysis of the Future of Blockchain and Digital Assets

The future of blockchain and digital assets appears promising, especially in the context of decentralized finance (DeFi) and other applications. Blockchain's inherent transparency and security make it a foundation for trustless systems. DeFi, leveraging smart contracts on blockchain, has the potential to revolutionize traditional finance by providing more accessible, efficient, and inclusive financial services.

Additionally, blockchain's impact extends beyond finance, with applications in supply chain management, healthcare, and voting systems. As technology evolves, scalability and interoperability challenges are being addressed, enhancing blockchain's utility and mainstream adoption.

As global interest continues to surge, cryptocurrencies offer a lifeline to those in developing nations, where conventional banking infrastructure faces limitations. The trends, opportunities, and potential risks paint a compelling picture – cryptocurrency is not just a passing trend; it's the future of currency.

Discussion of the Potential Trends and Developments in the Cryptocurrency Market

Cryptocurrency, has gained traction across the globe, becoming one of the most interesting investment vehicle in the past decade. In 2023, major trends include continued growth, corporate involvement, regulatory scrutiny, and the rise of DeFi.

Cryptocurrencies offer diverse investment alternatives, potential for significant returns, and transformative applications beyond banking. To navigate uncertainties, expert advice is crucial, addressing concerns such as regulatory risks, market volatility, and security issues.

Cryptocurrencies, with their decentralization, transparency, and global accessibility, are poised to revolutionize money usage. Despite challenges, the trends, opportunities, and potential risks suggest that cryptocurrencies are poised to become the currency of the future.

However, regulatory developments will significantly influence the trajectory of blockchain and digital assets. Striking a balance between innovation and regulatory compliance is crucial for sustained growth. The maturation of standards and frameworks is essential to establish a robust foundation for the broader integration of blockchain technologies.

In the ever-evolving financial landscape, traditional assets have played a crucial role in shaping personal and professional realms. Yet, the advent of technology and industrialization has propelled digital currencies to the forefront, with cryptocurrency emerging as a powerhouse transforming the financial landscapes for individuals and businesses alike. Let's unravel the captivating trends, navigate potential pitfalls, and explore the exciting future of cryptocurrency.

Overview of Emergency Blockchain Technologies and their Potential Impact

Emerging blockchain technologies exhibit diverse applications across industries. Polkadot aims to facilitate interoperability between blockchains, enhancing collaboration. Solana stands out for its high throughput, enabling rapid transaction processing. Avalanche focuses on decentralization and scalability, potentially reducing congestion issues. Algorand emphasizes efficiency through its consensus algorithm. These technologies hold promise for improved security, transparency, and efficiency in various sectors, from finance to supply chain management. As they mature, their impact on reshaping traditional processes and fostering innovation is likely to grow.

Explanation of Consensus Mechanism

Consensus mechanisms are crucial in blockchain, providing a shared foundation for decentralized networks to address disputes. They are protocols that synchronize all nodes on a blockchain, ensuring agreement on a single data set and validating transactions. Despite various mechanisms, they uniformly aim to deter cheating and maintain an immutable ledger.

Nodes input transaction data, receiving approval or disapproval after cross-checking with their records. Failure to adhere to consensus results in network bans. Challenges to records require network-wide approval, confirming and permanently writing the transaction into the blockchain.

In decentralized finance, consensus mechanisms replace centralized decision-making, validating transaction histories network-wide. Examples include proof of work, where miners authenticate transactions by solving computational puzzles, and proof of stake, where users stake tokens for a chance to verify transactions.

Consensus mechanisms are vital as fail-safes for blockchain, preventing double spending and ensuring trust. They incentivize good behavior, protecting against malicious activity and maintaining system integrity.

The five common consensus mechanisms are:

1. Proof of Work (PoW):
   - Pros: Highly decentralized and secure.
   - Cons: Slow transaction rates, high fees, and eco-hazardous energy usage.
   - Examples: Bitcoin, Dogecoin, Litecoin.

2. Proof of Stake (PoS):
   - Pros: Energy-efficient and cost-effective.
   - Cons: Less decentralized, power delegated by wallet size.
   - Examples: Ethereum, Cardano, Tezos, Algorand.

3. Delegated Proof of Stake (DPoS):
   - Pros: Efficient and democratic, financially inclusive.
   - Cons: Less decentralized, requires active engagement.
   - Examples: EOS, Lisk, Ark, Tron, BitShares, Steem.

4. Proof of Authority (PoA):
   - Pros: Highly scalable, minimal computing power.
   - Cons: Concentrated power, compromises decentralization.
   - Examples: Xodex, JP Morgan (JPMCoin), VeChain (VET), Ethereum Kovan testnet.

5. Proof of History (PoH):
   - Pros: Fast, secure, low transaction costs.
   - Cons: Accumulation of data, requires advanced hardware.
   - Examples: Solana.

Consensus mechanisms are not just technical safeguards; they establish trust in a trustless environment, preventing corruption and ensuring the blockchain operates in a decentralized manner. They are integral to the functionality and security of blockchain networks, offering diverse approaches to achieve a balance between decentralization, scalability, and security.

Investing in digital assets involves various strategies tailored to individual risk tolerance, goals, and market conditions. Here's a brief overview:

1. HODLing (Hold On for Dear Life): Long-term holding of digital assets with the belief that their value will increase over time. This strategy requires patience and a strong belief in the potential of the chosen assets.

2. Day Trading: Capitalizing on short-term price fluctuations by buying and selling within a single day. Day traders rely on technical analysis and market trends to make quick, frequent trades.

3. Swing Trading: Similar to day trading but with a slightly longer time horizon, typically days to weeks. Swing traders aim to capture "swings" in asset prices based on technical analysis and market trends.

4. Scalping: Extremely short-term trading aiming to profit from small price movements. Scalpers make numerous trades within a day, seeking to exploit market inefficiencies.

5. Dollar-Cost Averaging (DCA): Investing a fixed amount at regular intervals, regardless of the asset's price. This strategy aims to reduce the impact of market volatility over time.

6. Arbitrage: Exploiting price differences of the same asset on different exchanges or markets. This strategy requires quick execution and is more common in mature markets.

7. Staking and Yield Farming: Participating in blockchain networks by staking or providing liquidity to earn rewards. This involves locking up assets to support network operations.

8. ICO/IEO Participation: Investing in initial coin offerings (ICOs) or initial exchange offerings (IEOs) to get early access to new digital assets. This strategy carries higher risk due to the speculative nature of early-stage projects.

9. Research-Driven Investing: Thoroughly researching and analyzing digital assets before investing. This strategy focuses on understanding the technology, team, use case, and market potential of a project.

10. Sector and Theme Investing: Focusing on specific sectors or themes within the digital asset space, such as decentralized finance (DeFi), non-fungible tokens (NFTs), or blockchain interoperability.

It's crucial to diversify your portfolio, stay informed about market trends, and only invest what you can afford to lose. Additionally, consider factors like regulatory developments and security when formulating your digital asset investment strategy.

Explanation of fundamental and technical analysis

Exploring asset analysis methods for trading, two primary strategies are technical analysis and fundamental analysis. Let's first have a brief explanation of what fundamental and technical analysis are...

Technical analysis looks at patterns in market data to identify trends and predict how markets might move in the future. Fundamental analysis is a "big picture" approach that examines financials, user community, and future real-world utility.

Technical analysis delves into an asset's historical market performance, examining price trends and trading volume to gauge market sentiment and activity. On the other hand, fundamental analysis takes a big-picture approach, considering an asset's financials, user community, and real-world applications.

Fundamental analysis assesses intrinsic value, helping determine if an asset is over or underpriced. For example, Ethereum's value might rise if decentralized finance applications on its blockchain grow.

Technical analysis relies on current market prices and trading activity, assuming they reflect all known information. It captures market sentiment, aiding in trend prediction and investment decisions.

Combining both strategies provides a comprehensive view of trades, with fundamental analysis focusing on objective indicators for long-term value, while technical analysis concentrates on market performance.

Professional traders may lean toward one approach but often use both for a holistic perspective. Technical analysis, especially with computer models, aids in identifying short-term cycles for potential investment opportunities.

It's crucial to recognize the challenges of executing successful short-term strategies, especially in volatile markets. History doesn't always repeat, and studying price patterns may not guarantee accurate predictions.

Invest wisely and only what you can afford. Consult a financial advisor to develop a strategy and understand risks associated with cryptocurrency investments.

Comparison of Different Investment Approaches, including buy and hold, dollar-cost averaging, and trading

Let's have a brief comparison of different investment approaches:

1. Buy and Hold:
    - Strategy: Purchase investments and hold them for the long term.
    - Pros: Requires less active management, benefits from long-term market growth.
    - Cons: Vulnerable to market downturns, may miss short-term opportunities.

2. Dollar-Cost Averaging (DCA):
    - Strategy: Invest a fixed amount regularly, regardless of market conditions.
    - Pros: Reduces the impact of market volatility, disciplined approach.
    - Cons: May miss out on lump-sum investment gains during market lows.

3. Trading:
    - Strategy: Actively buy and sell securities to capitalize on short-term price movements.
    - Pros: Potential for quick profits, flexibility to react to market changes.
    - Cons: Requires significant time, and knowledge, and can be riskier due to market fluctuations and transaction costs.

Before you choose which to go with, you may need to consider a few areas, including:

- Risk Tolerance: Buy and hold suits those with high-risk tolerance, while trading requires a more active and risk-aware approach.

- Time Horizon: Buy and hold is ideal for long-term investors, while trading is often short-term focused.

- Discipline: Dollar-cost averaging enforces disciplined investing, while trading requires constant monitoring and decision-making.

- Costs: Trading can incur higher transaction costs, impacting overall returns compared to buy and hold or DCA.

Ultimately, the choice depends on your individual goals, risk tolerance, and the level of involvement you wish to have in managing their investments.

Overview of taxation and regulations of digital assets

Taxation and regulations regarding digital assets vary by country and are subject to frequent changes. Generally, digital assets, including cryptocurrencies, are considered taxable in many jurisdictions. Here's a broad overview:

1. Taxation:

   - *Capital Gains:* Profits from buying and selling digital assets are often treated as capital gains, and taxes apply accordingly.
   - *Income Tax:* Some countries tax digital asset transactions as ordinary income.
   - *Mining and Staking:* Income from mining or staking may be subject to taxation.
   - *Reporting Obligations*: Many jurisdictions require individuals to report digital asset holdings and transactions for tax purposes.

2. Regulations:

   - *AML/KYC Regulations*: Anti-Money Laundering (AML) and Know Your Customer (KYC) regulations are often applied to digital asset exchanges to prevent illicit activities.
   - *Securities Laws:* Some digital assets may be classified as securities, subjecting them to additional regulations.
   - *Licensing*: Exchanges and wallet providers may need licenses to operate legally.
   - *Consumer Protection*: Regulations aim to protect consumers by ensuring fair practices and disclosures.
   - *International Cooperation*: Many countries are working on international cooperation to address cross-border issues related to digital assets.

3. Global Variances:

   - *Divergent Approaches*: Different countries have varying approaches to classifying and taxing digital assets.
   - *Evolution of Regulations*: Regulations are evolving rapidly as governments adapt to the dynamic nature of the digital asset space.

4. Compliance:

   - *Compliance Challenges:* Adhering to regulations poses challenges for businesses in the digital asset space due to the evolving nature of the technology.

Future Developments:

There are ongoing changes, hence we expect continuous updates and changes in regulations as governments worldwide grapple with the complexities of digital assets. For example, Central Bank Digital Currencies (CBDCs) may introduce new regulatory frameworks in the future.

It's, therefore, crucial for individuals and businesses involved in digital assets to stay informed about the specific regulations in their jurisdictions and seek professional advice for compliance.

The cryptocurrency market encounters a myriad of regulatory challenges that stem from its decentralized nature and rapid evolution. One key issue is the uncertainty surrounding the classification of cryptocurrencies—whether they should be treated as commodities, currencies, securities, or a unique asset class. This ambiguity hampers regulatory efforts to create comprehensive frameworks.

Furthermore, the decentralized and pseudonymous nature of many cryptocurrencies raises concerns about their potential use in illicit activities such as money laundering and terrorism financing. Striking a balance between privacy and regulatory oversight is a delicate task that authorities grapple with globally.

Investor protection is another focal point. Market volatility, fraud, and hacking incidents underscore the need for robust safeguards to ensure the well-being of investors. Crafting regulations that address these risks without stifling innovation poses a significant challenge.

International coordination is crucial in addressing these issues, given the global nature of the cryptocurrency market. Harmonizing regulatory approaches can enhance effectiveness and reduce regulatory arbitrage.

Why DeFi is Important

Decentralized Finance (DeFi), reshaping global finance, offers accessibility worldwide due to its permissionless nature, operating 24/7 and enabling seamless transactions without intermediaries. Users benefit from financial sovereignty, controlling assets with transparency through open-source protocols. However, investing involves risks such as smart contract vulnerabilities, lack of insurance, and collateralization pitfalls.

Smart contract audits are crucial to mitigate vulnerabilities, and decentralized insurance solutions are emerging. Managing collateralization ratios is essential to prevent liquidation risks. Diligent research, diversification, and responsible risk management are vital for DeFi investors.

DeFi faces regulatory challenges, navigating a legal grey area due to the rapid evolution of the sector surpassing regulatory frameworks. Governments worldwide strive to balance innovation and consumer protection, working on regulatory guidelines for DeFi's safe growth. For example, FTX collapsed after it incurred multibillion-dollar losses. Seeking financing to bridge the approximately $8 billion gap between obligations and available funds, FTX, on Nov. 8, halted customer withdrawals, leaving hundreds of thousands without access to their funds. Unable to meet the $8 billion deficit, the company subsequently filed for bankruptcy, attributing the crash to fund mismanagement, liquidity issues, and a surge in withdrawals.

Looking ahead, DeFi's transformative impact continues to democratize financial services, enhance efficiency, and promote financial sovereignty. To reach its full potential, addressing scalability, user-friendliness, and security is key. Advancements in blockchain and Layer-2 solutions tackle scalability, while improvements in user interfaces make DeFi more accessible. As DeFi matures, integration with traditional finance is expected, creating a more inclusive and efficient financial ecosystem.

ROBO-ADVISORS FOR DIGITAL ASSETS

Explanation of Robo-Advisors and their role in investing

A robo-advisor is a digital platform that delivers automated, algorithm-driven financial planning and investment services with minimal human supervision. A standard robo-advisor inquires about your financial situation and future goals through an online survey, utilizing the gathered data to provide advice and automatically manage your investments.

Alternative terms for robo-advisors include "automated investment advisor," "automated investment management," and "digital advice platforms."

Top-tier robo-advisors provide straightforward account setup, robust goal planning, account services, and portfolio management. Additionally, they incorporate security features, and extensive education, and maintain low fees.

Overview of robo-advisors for digital assets

Robo-advisors for digital assets represent a revolutionary approach to investment management by leveraging automated, algorithmic processes with minimal human oversight. These platforms excel in implementing passive indexing strategies, aligning with the principles of modern portfolio theory to optimize portfolios based on risk tolerance and financial goals. The key advantage lies in their affordability, making them accessible to retail investors with low opening balance requirements.

Ideal for traditional investing, robo-advisors shine in managing diversified portfolios and rebalancing assets efficiently. However, their suitability diminishes when confronted with more intricate financial tasks like estate planning, where the nuances of individual circumstances often require personalized human guidance.

Despite their cost-effectiveness and efficiency, robo-advisors face criticism for perceived shortcomings. Critics highlight concerns about the lack of empathy inherent in automated systems and the potential oversimplification of complex financial matters. These critiques underscore the ongoing debate about striking the right balance between the efficiency of algorithmic solutions and the nuanced, personalized insights that human advisors can bring to certain financial situations. Nonetheless, for those seeking accessible and automated investment management, robo-advisors continue to represent a compelling option in the digital asset landscape.

Comparison of different robo-advisors for digital assets

So, you might be wondering if there are any robo-advisors out there that fit well with digital assets investing.

Here's a brief comparison of some of the most popular robo-advisors in the market today:

1. Wealthfront:
   - Crypto Exposure: 10%
   - Location: US-based

2. eToro:
   - Specialty: Best social investing platform
   - Crypto Features: Copy crypto investors or invest in crypto portfolios
   - Location: Not specified, but known globally

3. Makara:
   - Crypto Nature: 100% crypto-focused
   - Ownership: Affiliated with Betterment
   - Location: Not specified

4. Cryptosimple:
   - Region: European
   - Crypto Portfolio: Diversified with stable and volatile coins

5. Sarwa:
   - Crypto Exposure: 5% indirectly
   - Location: Not specified

6. M1 Finance:
   - Specialty: US-based
   - Crypto Access: Provides access to crypto and blockchain ETFs

7. Shrimpy Advisory:
   - Type: Newly launched cryptocurrency robo-advisor
   - User Base: Suitable for both beginners and experts
   - Diversity: Invests in various sectors of crypto

Note: It's important to consider factors like geographical restrictions, the extent of crypto exposure, platform usability, and user preferences when choosing a Crypto Robo-Advisor.

Explanation of how robo-advisors work in the cryptocurrency market

Robo-advisors have emerged as a revolutionary force in the digital investment landscape, leveraging sophisticated algorithms to streamline and automate the investment process for individuals. One of their key features is portfolio management, where they construct optimal portfolios based on investors' preferences. Employing some variant of the Modern Portfolio Theory, these digital platforms allocate funds to a mix of risky and risk-free assets, taking into consideration the investor's goals and risk profile.

The Modern Portfolio Theory emphasizes the diversification of assets, selecting stocks that are not perfectly positively correlated. This approach aims to optimize returns while managing risk. Furthermore, robo-advisors continually monitor and rebalance portfolios as economic conditions evolve. By adjusting the weights of risky and risk-free assets, they ensure that the portfolio remains aligned with the investor's objectives.

Another notable feature is tax-loss harvesting, a strategy employed to minimize capital gains tax. Towards the end of the tax year, robo-advisors automatically execute the sale of securities at a loss, allowing investors to offset capital gains. Simultaneously, they reinvest in similar securities to maintain the portfolio's overall allocation. This automated process not only saves on taxes but also ensures that the investor continues to benefit from market upturns.

Advantages and disadvantages of using robo-advisors for digital asset investing

Just like any other tool, robo-advisors have both advantages and disadvantages that may determine whether you'll go with it as part of your tools for digital investing.

Robo-advisors have reshaped the investment landscape by providing cost-effective and automated solutions. Their features, from portfolio management grounded in financial theories to tax-loss harvesting and user-friendly interfaces, cater to a broad spectrum of investors. While they lack the personalized touch of human advisors, robo-advisors offer a compelling option for those seeking accessible, low-cost investment management services with a level of customization based on individual risk preferences.

Here is a summary of the advantages and disadvantages of using robo-advisors in your digital investment journey:

Advantages of Robo-Advisors

1. Cost-effective investment management.

2. Lower fees compared to human financial advisors.

3. Minimal investment requirement, contrasting traditional financial planners.

4. User-friendly experience through mobile apps or web platforms.

5. Accessibility extends to portfolio management tools, ensuring flexibility and security.

6. Tailored portfolios based on individual risk preferences.

Disadvantages of Robo-Advisors

1. Lack of subjectivity for fully personalized services.

2. Absence of nuanced understanding compared to human advisors.

3. Regular check-ins and adjustments based on market changes are not inherent.

4. Debate with human advisors on expertise, management, and execution.

5. Sacrifice of expertise and personalization for cost-effective solutions.

6. Safety is dependent on investor preferences for risk and timeline.

Comparatively, the debate between robo-advisors and human advisors centers on expertise, management, and execution. Human advisors, with their subjective approach, charge higher fees and commissions. On the other hand, robo-advisors provide cost-effective solutions with more flexibility and control for investors but sacrifice the expertise and personalization offered by their human counterparts.

In addressing the safety of robo-advisors, it's crucial to recognize that their safety is neither absolute nor risky. The riskiness of a portfolio managed by a robo-advisor depends entirely on the investor's preferences. These platforms offer a range of risk and timeline preferences, enabling investors to choose portfolios aligned with their risk tolerance. Whether an investor opts for a riskier portfolio with more stocks or a more conservative one with a higher concentration of risk-free securities, robo-advisors tailor portfolios to meet individual appetites for risk.

In the cryptocurrency market, robo-advisors play a crucial role in the digital investment landscape. By utilizing automated algorithms, they streamline financial planning services without human intervention, gathering client data through online surveys to inform investment decisions.

While robo-advisors in the cryptocurrency space can generate profits like traditional financial advisors, their passive index investing strategies often aim to replicate market returns. Although they might not consistently outperform the market, robo-advisors optimize risk-return tradeoffs based on modern portfolio theory.

Despite the potential for losses if investments decline or costs exceed returns, robo-advisors offer benefits like automated portfolio management, rebalancing, and tax-loss harvesting. These features were once complex or costly for ordinary investors but are now made accessible through algorithmic trading and electronic markets.

With low fees and minimal initial investment requirements, robo-advisors are particularly appealing to long-term investors, especially younger individuals who embrace technology. In the cryptocurrency market, their integration into a digital investment strategy reflects the broader trend of leveraging automation for efficient and cost-effective portfolio management.

To create a winning digital investing strategy using robo-advisors in the cryptocurrency market, you can follow these steps:

1. Assess Risk Tolerance:
   - Begin by completing the online survey provided by the robo-advisor to determine your risk tolerance and investment goals.

2. Set Investment Objectives:
   - Clearly define your investment objectives, whether it's long-term wealth accumulation, retirement planning, or specific financial goals.

3. Portfolio Customization:
   - Utilize the robo-advisor's tools to customize your portfolio based on your risk appetite and preferences. Modern portfolio theory will guide the allocation of assets for an optimal risk-return balance.

4. Automated Investing:
   - Leverage the robo-advisor's automated algorithms to execute your investment strategy. This ensures consistent and disciplined execution without emotional decision-making.

5. Regular Monitoring:

- Regularly review your investment portfolio and adjust your strategy if your financial goals or risk tolerance change. Robo-advisors often provide automated rebalancing to maintain the desired asset allocation.

6. Tax-Efficient Strategies:

- Take advantage of tax-efficient strategies offered by robo-advisors, such as tax-loss harvesting. This can help optimize your tax liabilities and enhance overall returns.

7. Stay Informed:

- Stay informed about the cryptocurrency market trends and developments. While robo-advisors automate many processes, being aware of market dynamics can inform your overall investment strategy.

8. Diversification:

- Emphasize diversification within your portfolio to spread risk across various assets. Robo-advisors, often following passive index strategies, can assist in achieving a well-diversified portfolio.

9. Long-Term Perspective:

- Adopt a long-term investment perspective. Cryptocurrency markets can be volatile, and robo-advisors are well-suited for investors with a patient, long-term approach.

10. Tech-Forward Approach:

- If you're a tech-forward investor, appreciate the accessibility and user-friendly interfaces provided by robo-advisors. They cater to a digital-savvy audience with low fees and minimum balance requirements.

By integrating these steps, you can leverage robo-advisors in the cryptocurrency market to create a winning digital investing strategy. This approach combines the benefits of automation, risk management, and cost efficiency to navigate the dynamic landscape of digital assets.

Analysis of the potential for robo-advisors to disrupt the traditional investment industry

Robo-advisors have emerged as a disruptive force in the traditional investment landscape, fundamentally altering the way individuals approach portfolio management. At the core of this transformation lies the utilization of algorithms, which automate and streamline the investment process. While the current consensus suggests that artificial intelligence (AI) is not a predominant factor in robo-advisory platforms, some trailblazing firms, such as Wealthfront, have begun incorporating AI into their offerings.

Wealthfront, for instance, has introduced a tool called "Path," which goes beyond traditional robo-advisory functionalities. This feature utilizes AI to answer complex financial questions, such as determining the optimal retirement age or identifying affordable neighborhoods. By incorporating AI into these supplementary features, robo-advisors like Wealthfront enhance their value proposition, moving beyond mere portfolio management to address broader financial planning concerns.

The evolving landscape of exchange-traded funds (ETFs) further complicates the relationship between robo-advisors and AI. As the ETF market undergoes a transformation fueled by AI applications, it raises questions about the role of AI within robo-advisory platforms. The increasing sophistication and profitability of AI-driven strategies in the ETF space could potentially reduce the incentive for robo-advisors to develop and maintain their own AI algorithms.

A plausible scenario is the shift of focus from creating proprietary AI-driven strategies to leveraging AI-enhanced ETFs. This pivot allows robo-advisors to benefit from the advancements in AI without the need for in-house development. Investing in these AI-driven ETFs not only aligns with the industry trend but also offers a more efficient and cost-effective approach for robo-advisors to deliver returns to their clients.

While AI's presence in the robo-advisory sector may not be widespread at present, its potential future impact is a critical consideration. The nascent integration of AI, as seen in tools like Wealthfront's "Path," showcases the industry's willingness to explore and incorporate advanced technologies for a more comprehensive financial experience. As AI continues to evolve and permeate various facets of the financial sector, robo-advisors may find new opportunities to enhance their offerings, providing investors with a more sophisticated and personalized approach to wealth management.

Case studies of successful robo-advisor platforms in the cryptocurrency market.

Wealthfront:

Wealthfront stands out as the best overall robo-advisor for 2023, excelling in goal planning and portfolio management. Offering sophisticated financial planning, customized portfolios, and up to $1 million FDIC insurance, Wealthfront's mobile app matches the functionality of its desktop version seamlessly. With fees at 0.25% for most accounts, no trading commissions, and no fees for withdrawals, minimums, or transfers, Wealthfront maintains a competitive edge with a minimum account requirement of $500, earning an impressive Investopedia rating of 4.9/5.

Betterment:

For beginners and those seeking robust cash management features, Betterment proves to be an excellent choice. The platform offers customizable asset allocation, the ability to create multiple goals, and scenario testing for those goals. With fees at 0.25% annually for investing plan accounts meeting specific criteria, or $4/month otherwise, Betterment's low initial investment requirement of $10 makes it accessible to a wide range of investors. Its Investopedia rating of 4.6/5 reflects its user-friendly interface and comprehensive features.

M1 Finance:

Recognized as the best robo-advisor for low costs and appealing to sophisticated investors, M1 Finance boasts low-cost, customizable portfolios. With a vast list of prebuilt portfolios and options for borrowing and spending, M1 Finance charges no management fees. The platform's account minimum is $100, with a slightly higher requirement of $500 for retirement accounts. While it earns a rating of 4.3/5 on Investopedia, its emphasis on cost-effectiveness and flexibility makes it an attractive choice for investors.

Merrill Guided Investing:

Merrill Guided Investing stands out for its educational focus, offering easy navigation, superb goal-planning tools, and calculators. Customers benefit from Preferred Rewards, helping reduce fees, and portfolios managed by financial experts. With fees at 0.45% of assets under management (0.85% with an advisor) and discounts available for Bank of America Preferred Rewards participants, Merrill Guided Investing requires a minimum investment of $1,000. Its Investopedia rating of 4.6/5 reflects its commitment to customer education and service.

E*TRADE:

Tailored for mobile-first investors, E*TRADE earns recognition for its mobile accessibility and socially responsible investing options. With fees at 0.30% and a reasonable account minimum of $500, E*TRADE caters to newer investors seeking a user-friendly platform. While it earns a solid Investopedia rating of 4.1/5, E*TRADE's focus on mobile functionality makes it a standout choice for investors on the go.

Chapter 10- Fractional Investing and Tokenization This chapter will provide readers with an understanding of how fractional investing and tokenization can increase accessibility and democratize investing in the cryptocurrency market. It will highlight the benefits and drawbacks of these strategies and provide real-world examples of successful platforms in the industry. The chapter will also discuss the potential for tokenization to unlock value in traditionally illiquid assets, and provide insights into the future of these strategies in the cryptocurrency market. Explanation of Fractional investing and its benefits Fractional ownership, a modern investment approach, has emerged as an innovative solution that democratizes access to high-value assets and provides a pathway for individuals to diversify their investment portfolios. At its core, fractional ownership enables investors to purchase a percentage or share of an asset, such as real estate, fine art, or even high-end yachts, without the need for substantial capital. One of the primary benefits of fractional ownership is its ability to lower the financial commitment required for investment. This model breaks down the barriers that traditionally limited individuals with less access to capital from entering the realm of high-value asset ownership. By allowing investors to buy into a fraction of an asset, the financial burden is distributed among multiple participants, making it a feasible option for a broader range of investors. The process of fractional ownership typically involves a sponsor or manager forming a legal ownership entity that acquires the desired asset, whether it's a vacation home, a private jet, or a piece of artwork. This entity then divides the ownership rights into shares, which are sold to individual investors. This approach not only raises capital but also spreads the financial responsibility among co-owners. In addition to acquiring equity in the asset, fractional owners may also gain partial usage rights, depending on the specific terms of the fractional agreement. For example, someone engaged in fractional ownership of a vacation property might have the opportunity to use the space personally and earn revenue when it is rented out during periods of non-personal use. This added flexibility enhances the appeal of fractional ownership as an investment strategy. The involvement of legal entities like limited partnerships or limited liability companies further formalizes the structure of fractional ownership. This legal framework ensures that economic returns, whether from usage fees, rentals, or sales, are distributed according to ownership percentages. It also centralizes management control with the sponsor or general partner, providing a streamlined approach to decision-making and ongoing operations. Beyond the financial benefits, fractional ownership offers a unique avenue for diversification. Investors can spread their risk across different types of assets, from luxury real estate to high-end yachts, thereby reducing the impact of market fluctuations on their overall portfolio. This diversification potential adds an extra layer of appeal for those seeking a balanced and resilient investment strategy. Moreover, fractional ownership presents the opportunity for appreciation and income generation. In real estate, for instance, fractional properties can appreciate over time, potentially resulting in capital gains for investors. Additionally, when these properties are not in personal use, owners may generate income by renting them out. Overview of tokenization and how it works Tokenization is a security measure replacing sensitive data, like credit card details, with unique symbols called tokens. The goal is to keep essential information intact while reducing the risk associated with storing sensitive data. It's widely used in credit card transactions, e-commerce, and beyond, offering a way for businesses to enhance security and comply with regulations. In this process, tokens act as stand-ins for sensitive information. They can be generated using reversible cryptographic functions, nonreversible hash functions, or random indexes. The key aspect is that these tokens become visible information, while the actual sensitive data is kept safe in a central storage known as a token vault. Only within this vault can the original information be traced back to its corresponding token. For instance, when a customer provides payment details at a store or online checkout, these details are replaced by a randomly generated token. This tokenized information is then encrypted and sent to a payment processor. The original sensitive payment information resides securely in a token vault within the merchant's system. The vault serves as the exclusive place where the token can be linked back to the actual information. Some tokenization methods are vaultless, meaning they don't rely on a secure database. Instead, tokens are stored using algorithms. This approach, particularly when tokens are reversible, offers flexibility without the need for a dedicated storage vault. Overall, tokenization provides a robust solution to safeguard sensitive data in various domains, emphasizing security without compromising operational efficiency. Comparison of traditional investing to fractional investing and tokenization Traditional real estate investment and fractional real estate investment represent two distinct paradigms with unique attributes, catering to diverse investor preferences and goals. In the realm of traditional real estate investment, the cornerstone is direct ownership. Investors acquire physical properties such as residential homes or commercial buildings, either individually or in collaboration with others. This method demands a substantial capital outlay, covering property acquisition, down payments, maintenance, and active property management. While it affords investors significant control over decisions, it also entails responsibilities like tenant interactions, maintenance, and coping with property value fluctuations. Conversely, fractional real estate investment involves an indirect ownership structure. Investors purchase shares or units in real estate assets through trusts, partnerships, or platforms. The capital requirements are comparatively lower, making this approach more accessible. However, it relinquishes some control to an asset manager or platform, leading to passive involvement for investors. The appeal of fractional investment lies in its ability to facilitate enhanced diversification. By allowing investors to spread their capital across multiple properties or locations, it mitigates concentration risk. Liquidity is another differentiating factor. Traditional real estate investments often lack immediate liquidity, requiring time-consuming processes for property sales. In contrast, fractional investments are more liquid, enabling easier buying and selling through online platforms or secondary markets. While traditional investments may yield higher rental income, fractional investments provide a potential for steady income through regular distributions. Risk and responsibility are also distributed differently, with traditional investors bearing direct responsibility, while fractional investors share it with others and the overseeing entity. Ultimately, the choice between these approaches hinges on individual circumstances, risk tolerance, and investment objectives. Some investors might find value in blending both methods to strike a balance between control, accessibility, and diversification in their real estate portfolios. Analysis of how fractional investing and tokenization can increase accessibility to digital assets Fractional investing and tokenization play pivotal roles in democratizing access to digital assets. Tokenization, particularly of real-world assets, revolutionizes traditional financial markets by enabling fractional ownership, increasing liquidity, and fostering broader accessibility.

1. Fractional Ownership: Tokenization allows individuals to own fractions of high-value assets, such as commercial properties, making investments more accessible. This democratization of ownership expands investment opportunities for a diverse range of investors.

2. Increased Liquidity: Tokenization addresses the historical challenge of liquidity in traditionally illiquid markets. Digital asset tokens can be traded 24/7 on global exchanges, reducing transaction time and costs associated with buying or selling assets.

3. Transparency: Blockchain ensures transparent and immutable ownership records, enhancing trust and reducing the potential for fraudulent activities. This transparency is crucial for investors and contributes to a more reliable financial ecosystem.

4. Efficiency in Financial Markets: The digitalization and tokenization of assets bring efficiency by reducing intermediaries like custodians and brokers, thereby lowering transaction costs. Smart contracts automate settlements, significantly reducing settlement times and counterparty risks. Global accessibility is heightened as digital assets are available to anyone with an internet connection, breaking down geographical barriers and expanding investment opportunities globally.

5. Opportunities for Brands and Enterprises: Security Token Offerings (STOs) provide an efficient means for businesses to raise capital, especially beneficial for startups and smaller enterprises.

   Brands can engage customers through utility tokens and loyalty rewards on blockchain platforms, fostering brand loyalty and customer participation in token-based ecosystems.

6. Regulatory and Security Considerations: Despite the transformative potential, addressing regulatory and security concerns is crucial to fully unlock the benefits of digital assets. Striking the right balance between innovation and compliance is essential for the sustainable growth of this ecosystem.

In summary, embracing fractional investing and tokenization has the potential to reshape the financial landscape, democratize finance, and create innovative opportunities for brands and enterprises. Careful navigation of regulatory challenges will be key to realizing the full potential of digital assets in fostering financial innovation and inclusivity. Discussion of the potential for fractional investing and tokenization to democratize investing Tokenization, driven by blockchain technology, is transforming the investment landscape by democratizing access to capital and breaking down traditional barriers. Through fractional ownership, investors can now participate in assets like real estate, fine art, or music royalties with smaller denominations, promoting diversity and inclusivity in previously exclusive markets. This accessibility not only enables a broader range of investors but also unlocks liquidity in traditionally illiquid assets, allowing for risk reduction and higher returns. The borderless nature of tokenization facilitates cross-border investment opportunities, eliminating geographical barriers and empowering investors to tap into promising markets worldwide. The reduction of complexities associated with international investments promotes global capital flows and fosters economic growth. Blockchain's decentralized and immutable ledger enhances transparency and accountability in the investment process. Every transaction involving tokenized assets is recorded and verifiable, reducing the potential for fraudulent activities. Smart contracts, based on blockchain technology, automate investment processes, eliminating intermediaries, reducing costs, expediting settlement times, and increasing overall efficiency in the investment ecosystem. The democratization of investment opportunities extends beyond traditional assets to alternative asset classes, including startups and small businesses. Tokenization allows entities to raise capital through ICOs or STOs, providing a viable alternative to traditional fundraising methods. This approach opens up investment opportunities for a wider pool of investors, fosters innovation, and supports the growth of disruptive ventures. As we embrace tokenization, we embark on a journey toward a more inclusive and accessible financial future. Fractional investing and tokenization revolutionize the investment landscape, offering unprecedented opportunities for the next generation of innovators and entrepreneurs, ultimately paving the way for a more secure, transparent, and efficient investment ecosystem. Explanation of how tokenization can unlock value in illiquid assets Tokenization serves as a transformative force in unlocking value within traditionally illiquid assets, ushering in a new era of accessibility and democratization in the financial landscape. The process involves digitizing the proof of ownership of real-world assets, essentially creating blockchain tokens that represent ownership rights. This digital representation brings about a myriad of advantages, particularly in addressing the liquidity challenges faced by assets like real estate, art, and collectibles. Illiquid assets, by their nature, often entail prolonged processes for selling or renting, hindered by regulatory complexities, geographical constraints, and inherent time lags. Tokenization disrupts this status quo by fractionalizing ownership. Through platforms like RealT, investors can own a fraction of a property without the usual substantial down payment, instantly enhancing liquidity. This means enjoying monthly rental income without navigating the intricacies of real estate transactions through agents or intermediaries. The scope of tokenization extends beyond real estate to encompass various asset classes. Gold, music royalties, whisky, and equity have all undergone tokenization, offering investors diverse opportunities for portfolio diversification. Each tokenized asset comes with its unique benefits, such as Paxos Gold and Tether Gold ensuring each gold token is backed by physical gold, or ANote Music allowing investors to profit from tokenized music dividends. Moreover, the transparency inherent in blockchain technology brings a new level of visibility to investors. Tokenized assets' data, including appraisal values, income, occupancy, expenses, and cap tables, is fully accessible on the blockchain. This transparency not only builds trust but also allows investors to make informed decisions, splitting risks and co-owning physical assets with individuals they may have never met. In essence, tokenization represents a revolution in financial markets, not only enhancing liquidity but also democratizing access to capital markets. The permanence of this revolution is underscored by the projected growth of the Asset Tokenization market to $16 trillion and 10% of the GDP by 2030, as predicted by the Boston Consulting Group. Platforms like RealT are already paving the way for individuals to forge their paths in decentralized finance, marking a paradigm shift in the way we perceive and interact with traditional assets. Case studies of successful fractional investing and tokenization platforms in the cryptocurrency market These case studies highlight some successful implementations of asset tokenization across various asset classes. 1. RealT: RealT is a platform that tokenizes real estate, allowing users to invest in fractional ownership of properties. It provides an opportunity for smaller investors to access the real estate market with lower entry costs. 2. Myco: Myco offers fractional investing in art and collectibles through tokenization. This platform enables art enthusiasts to own a share of valuable artworks, making art investment more accessible. 3. Rarible: Rarible is a decentralized marketplace that enables users to tokenize and trade digital assets. Artists and creators can tokenize their work, allowing investors to buy and trade fractional ownership of digital assets. 4. Harbor: Harbor focuses on tokenizing traditional assets, including real estate and private equity. It provides a regulatory-compliant infrastructure for the issuance and trading of security tokens. These platforms showcase the growing trend of fractional investing and tokenization, making various asset classes more inclusive for a broader range of investors in the cryptocurrency market. Risks and challenges associated with fractional investing and tokenization Like any other venture, fractional investing and tokenization carries with it certain degree of risks to both creators and investors. Here, we highlight a few common risks you're likely to encounter as you navigate fractional investing and tokenization: 1. Regulatory Uncertainty: The lack of clear regulatory frameworks poses a significant risk to fractional investing and asset tokenization. Companies may face legal challenges and uncertainty regarding compliance with evolving regulations, hindering the widespread adoption of tokenization. 2. Liquidity Challenges: Token value is closely tied to market demand. Without a robust market, liquidity can be compromised, making it difficult for investors to sell tokens. Companies must assess market viability before tokenizing assets to prevent potential liquidity issues. 3. Security Vulnerabilities: Storing tokens on a decentralized blockchain exposes them to security threats. Hacking and cyberattacks pose risks to the integrity of tokenized assets. Companies must prioritize robust security measures to safeguard against potential breaches and protect investor interests. 4. Technology Reliability: Tokenization heavily relies on technology, introducing the risk of system failures. Technological glitches or breakdowns could result in asset loss or hinder the trading of tokens. Companies should implement reliable technology and contingency plans to mitigate these risks. 5. Lack of Standardization: The absence of industry standards in tokenization creates challenges in interoperability between different platforms. This lack of standardization can lead to confusion and hinder the seamless trading of tokens across various platforms, impacting investor confidence. In navigating these challenges, companies pursuing tokenization should prioritize comprehensive risk management strategies and stay attuned to evolving regulatory landscapes to ensure the sustainable and secure adoption of this transformative technology in the financial industry. Future potential of fractional investing and tokenization in the cryptocurrency market Fractional investing and tokenization in the cryptocurrency market have the potential to democratize access to a variety of assets. By breaking down assets into smaller, more affordable units, fractional investing allows a broader range of investors to participate in traditionally high-barrier markets, such as real estate or fine art. Tokenization takes this concept further by representing ownership of fractionalized assets as digital tokens on a blockchain. This enhances liquidity, transparency, and accessibility. Investors can trade these tokens easily, promoting a more efficient and inclusive financial ecosystem. In the future, fractional investing and tokenization could be implemented in the retail sector for retail investors to gain access to a broader range of asset classes. Additionally, tokenization may streamline traditionally complex processes like settlement and reduce the need for intermediaries, potentially lowering costs and increasing market efficiency. However, regulatory challenges and concerns regarding security and market manipulation need to be addressed for these technologies to reach their full potential.

GLOSSARY

Altcoin: Any cryptocurrency other than Bitcoin.

AML (Anti-Money Laundering): Regulations and measures aimed at preventing money laundering and illegal financial activities.

Arbitrage: Exploiting price differences of the same asset on different exchanges or markets.

Avalanche: Avalanche focuses on decentralization and scalability, potentially addressing congestion issues that some blockchains face. This could lead to more efficient and scalable blockchain solutions.

Blockchain: A distributed ledger technology that records transactions across multiple computers in a secure and transparent manner.

Capital gains: The profit earned from the sale of an asset.

Capital gains tax: A tax on the profit made from the sale of an asset.

CFTC (Commodity Futures Trading Commission): The regulatory agency overseeing derivatives markets and commodities trading in the United States.

Compliance: Adherence to legal and regulatory requirements.

Corporate Involvement: More companies are likely to get involved in the cryptocurrency space, whether by accepting cryptocurrencies as payment or by holding them as part of their treasury reserves.

Cryptography: The use of mathematical techniques to secure and protect data.

Crypto exposure: The percentage of an investment portfolio allocated to cryptocurrencies.

Decentralization: The distribution of control and decision-making across a network rather than a centralized authority.

DeFi (Decentralized Finance) Revolution: DeFi is expected to play a pivotal role in reshaping traditional finance. Its use of smart contracts and blockchain technology enables more accessible, efficient, and inclusive financial services. DeFi has the potential to democratize finance, making it accessible to individuals who were previously excluded from the traditional banking system.

Direct ownership: The traditional method of owning physical assets individually or in collaboration with others.

Diversification: Spreading investment capital across different assets or locations to reduce risk.

Double Spending: A potential issue in digital currencies where the same funds are spent more than once.

Exchange: A platform for buying and selling cryptocurrencies.

Exchange-traded funds (ETFs): Investment funds that are traded on stock exchanges, often designed to replicate the performance of a specific index.

Financial goals: The specific objectives an individual aims to achieve through financial planning and investing.

Financial planning: The process of setting financial goals, assessing resources, and creating a plan to achieve those goals.

FOMO (Fear of Missing Out): The fear that drives investors to enter the market due to the expectation of missing out on potential profits.

FUD (Fear, Uncertainty, Doubt): Negative information or rumors spread to create fear and uncertainty in the market.

Global Accessibility: Cryptocurrencies, as a subset of digital assets, offer a lifeline to individuals in developing nations where traditional banking infrastructure is limited. The global interest in cryptocurrencies suggests that they are not just a passing trend but the future of currency.

HODLing (Hold On for Dear Life): This strategy involves holding digital assets for the long term with the belief that their value will increase over time.

ICO (Initial Coin Offering): A fundraising method in which new cryptocurrencies are sold to investors.

Indirect ownership: An ownership structure where investors purchase shares or units in assets through trusts, partnerships, or platforms.

KYC (Know Your Customer): The process of verifying the identity of customers as required by financial institutions and regulators.

Liquidity: The ease with which an asset can be bought or sold without significantly affecting its price.

Market Capitalization: The total value of a cryptocurrency calculated by multiplying its price by its circulating supply.

Market Volatility: Cryptocurrency markets are known for their volatility, and this is expected to continue. Traders and investors should be prepared for price fluctuations and market swings.

Mining: The process of validating and recording transactions on a blockchain, often involving the solving of complex mathematical puzzles.

Modern Portfolio Theory (MPT): A theory that emphasizes diversification of assets to optimize returns while managing risk.

Polkadot: Polkadot aims to facilitate interoperability between blockchains, enabling them to work together more effectively. This could enhance collaboration and innovation in the blockchain space.

Portfolio customization: The process of tailoring an investment portfolio to align with an investor's risk appetite and preferences.

Proof of Authority (PoA): PoA relies on trusted validators or authorities to validate transactions. It is highly scalable but sacrifices decentralization.

Proof of History (PoH): PoH is used in Solana and provides a historical record of events on the blockchain to improve transaction processing speed.

Proof of Stake (PoS): PoS validators are chosen to create new blocks based on the number of cryptocurrency tokens they hold and are willing to "stake" as collateral.

Proof of Work (PoW): In PoW, miners solve complex computational puzzles to validate transactions and create new blocks. It is energy-intensive but highly secure.

Regulatory Authority: A government agency responsible for overseeing and enforcing regulations.

Regulatory Scrutiny: Regulatory bodies around the world are expected to increase their scrutiny of the cryptocurrency market. This could lead to the development of clearer regulatory frameworks and increased compliance requirements for crypto-related businesses.

Research-Driven Investing: In-depth research and analysis of digital assets before investing.

Rise of DeFi: DeFi is expected to expand further, offering a wider range of financial services and products to users. This could lead to increased adoption of DeFi protocols and platforms.

Rental income: Income generated from renting out properties or assets.

Robo-Advisor: A digital platform that provides automated financial planning and investment services using algorithms and minimal human supervision.

ROI (Return on Investment): A measure of the profitability of an investment, often expressed as a percentage.

Scalping: Extremely short-term trading aiming to profit from small price movements.

SEC (U.S. Securities and Exchange Commission): The regulatory body responsible for securities and financial markets in the United States.

Sector and Theme Investing: Focusing on specific sectors or themes within the digital asset space.

Security Token Offering (STO): A fundraising method in which digital tokens representing ownership in an asset or company are sold, typically complying with securities regulations.

Security tokenization: The process of converting ownership rights of an asset into digital tokens on a blockchain.

Smart Contracts: Self-executing contracts with the terms of the agreement directly written into code.

Solana: Solana is known for its high throughput, which allows for rapid transaction processing. This could make it suitable for applications that require quick and high-volume transactions.

Staking and Yield Farming: Earning rewards by participating in blockchain networks or providing liquidity.

Swing Trading: Like day trading but with a slightly longer time horizon, typically days to weeks.

Taxation: The process of imposing taxes on cryptocurrency transactions and holdings.

Token: A unique symbol used to represent sensitive data in tokenization.

Token vault: A secure storage for sensitive data in tokenization.

Tokenization: The process of converting ownership or rights to an asset into digital tokens, often to increase liquidity and accessibility.

User base: The group of individuals or investors who use a particular platform or service.

User preferences: Individual choices and preferences that influence investment decisions.

Utility Token: A token that provides access to a specific product or service within a blockchain ecosystem.

Vesting Period: A specified time during which tokens or shares are locked and cannot be sold.

Volatility: The degree of variation in the price of an asset over time.

ABOUT THE AUTHOR:

Cas Havis II is a dedicated finance professional with a strong background in blockchain technology, and this is his second self-published book in the field of digital currencies. With a career spanning both in the military and civilian sectors, Cas brings a unique blend of financial acumen and blockchain expertise to the modern financial landscape.

As a Cryptocurrency Consultant, Blogger, and Author since 2017, Cas has been on a mission to make cryptocurrency approachable and accessible to individuals worldwide. Through e-book sales and 1:1 consulting session, Cas has garnered rave reviews while helping clients embark on their cryptocurrency journey.

Cas's passion for the world of digital currencies is evident in his work. His first-hand experiences provide a unique perspective that enriches his writing. His expertise and dedication make him a trusted guide for anyone looking to navigate the complex world of digital assets.